Healthy Leaders Healthy Churches

You Cannot Lead Beyond Who You Really Are

FRANCIS BOLA AKIN-JOHN

Healthy Leaders, Healthy Churches

ISBN 978-941-4358

Copyright (c) 2008 Francis Bola Akin-John

All rights reserved. No part may be reproduced without the written permission of the publisher.

All Scripture quotations are from King James Version of the Bible, unless otherwise stated.

Published by:

CHURCH GROWTH SERVICES INC.
332, Abeokuta Expressway, By Super Bus Stop,
Oke-Odo, Agege, Lagos.
Tel.: 234-01-8976100, 08023000714, 08029744296
E-mail: akingrow@yahoo.com
www.churchgrowthafrica.org.

Printed in Nigeria by
LIFE & MINISTRY PUBLICATIONS
Tel.: 234-01-7934133, 08037152451

Healthy Leaders, Healthy Churches

Contents

Dedication	*5*
Appreciation	*7*

Introduction:
The Greatest Curse on people or Work 11

Chapter ONE:
Pastoring or Leading The Church Today
It is only the purest form of leadership that will work in the church 15

Chapter TWO:
The Rise and Fall of Churches
More than anybody else, leaders have the power to kill churches 29

Chapter THREE:
Weaknesses of Leaders That Weaken Churches
People don't really leave churches, they only leave leaders because of weaknesses. 45

Chapter FOUR:
Secret of Healthy Leadership: Lead Yourself First
You are the greatest crowd you will ever lead 61

Healthy Leaders, Healthy Churches

Chapter FIVE:
Capacity of Leaders, Capacity of Churches
When leaders stop improving, churches start decreasing   **79**

Chapter SIX:
Relationship: The Heart Of Leadership
If your relational skills are weak, your leader ship will always suffer   **91**

Chapter SEVEN:
Competent Pastoral Leaders Today
Incompetent leaders have done much more damage to the church.   **105**

Healthy Leaders, Healthy Churches

Dedication

I heartily dedicate this book
to the
growth, health and dynamism of
the body of Christ
in the world

Healthy Leaders, Healthy Churches

Dedication

Healthy Leaders, Healthy Churches

Appreciation

To my Ultimate Leader
- Mighty praise and thanks

To my co-workers
- Deep appreciation and love

To my family
- Eternal gratitude for your understanding

To my leaders
- Thanks for enduring with me

To my Mentorees
- Thanks for the opportunity to lead you

To my Readers
- Thanks for applying the truths

To my Printer
- Thank you for another great work

To my Critics
- Thanks for keeping me on my toes.

8/ Appreciation

Healthy Leaders, Healthy Churches

Healthy Leaders, Healthy Churches

BLESSED LEADERS

"Blessed are the ..." **(Matt. 5:3,4,5,6,7,8,9,10,11)**

1. Blessed are the leaders who lead themselves first, for they shall then be able to lead others well.

2. Blessed are the leaders who embrace a vision greater than themselves, for what they give their lives to will endure forever.

3. Blessed are the leaders who live each day with eternity in view, for in looking back on life, there will be no regrets.

4. Blessed are the leaders who continuously connect to the Ultimate Leader, for their source will not run dry.

5. Blessed are the leaders who keep on learning, for they shall fall into a reservoir of God's revelation.

6. Blessed are the leaders who place great value on people, for they shall not lack friends,

Healthy Leaders, Healthy Churches

partners and supporters.

7. Blessed are the leaders who can smile and laugh at themselves, for they shall not cease to be entertained.

8. Blessed are the leaders who serve with a caring, loving and servant heart, for they shall have results that will astound them.

9. Blessed are the leaders who keep on working on themselves, for their weaknesses will not weaken their work.

10. Blessed are the leaders who invest in emerging leaders, for their work will not die with them.

11. Blessed are the leaders who lead their homes well, for they shall have the credibility to lead the people of God.

12. Blessed are the leaders who embrace change, improvement and development, for they shall not grow stale and be rejected.

13. Blessed are the leaders who release people to their ministries, for their work will multiply after them.

INTRODUCTION

The Greatest Curse On People Or Work

I must confess that it has taken me years to summon courage to write this book, simply because there are many excellent books and resources on leadership. Our foreign brothers and some African writers have done some good work on this interesting subject.

However, the burden and pressure to write have been very much on me lately because of the appalling situation of leadership in the African church. I have been privileged to visit, counsel and share with very many church leaders across denominational divides in the last fourteen years and I found out that the leadership challenge is always the same everywhere.

Thank God for the numerical growth of the church in Africa. But the sad news is that good, godly, dynamic and healthy leadership is abysmally low in our churches. The more reason churches rise and fall in quick succession in Africa. Our largest churches, be it Pentecostal, Charismatic or Traditional are suffering seriously from the malaise of sick and unwholesome leadership.

Healthy Leaders, Healthy Churches

From what I've seen so far, I'm afraid that our future is very bleak without healthy leaders rising to the surface. Without mincing words, the church in Nigeria, nay Africa, needs healthy leaders now more than ever before if we are going to conserve the harvest and go on to fulfill the great commission of our Lord.

I strongly believe that the greatest curse that can be placed on any group of people or work is that of bad, bogus and ungodly leadership. Once there is no true leadership, any nation, people and work is cursed. Unfortunately, this is the curse on Nigeria, Africa and sadly, the church.

"For behold, the Lord, the LORD of hosts doth take away from Jerusalem and from Judah ... the mighty man, the man of war, the judge, and the prophet, and the prudent, the ancient, the captain of fifty, the counselor, the honorable man, the artificer and the eloquent orator ... " (Isaiah 3:1-3; 4,5,12).

In this scripture, the Almighty God was unleashing one of the most terrible punishments anyone, nation or group of people could ever have. That is to have no leaders. If you look closely at this scripture, you will see that God was predicting the removal of every type of leader from the community. The situation described above is an indication of a headless society because every kind of leader is taken away. A nation, people, work and church without a real leader is cursed. And in place of real leaders, Jehovah predicted the rise of bogus leadership.

"And I will give children to be their princes, and babes shall rule over them ... "

These children and babies represent incapable and useless leaders. It is obvious that a baby cannot rule his own bowels, how much more rule a nation. What would be the result of having such junky and bogus leader? The Bible has the answers:

"The people shall be oppressed, everyone by another and everyone by his neighbor: the child shall behave himself proudly against the ancient, and the base against the honorable ... o my people, they which lead thee cause thee to err, and destroy the way of thy paths."

Almost every bad situation within the church can be attributed to the lack of good and healthy leader. Church splits and scandals are often the result of lack of strong leadership.

Churches and ministries rise and fall depending on their leadership. With bad and bogus leadership, the church will err and not go anywhere, even if many of our pastors are highly anointed.

From my interaction, research and deep observation of church leaders across Africa, I have come to discover that we have dynamic pastors, anointed preachers, powerful evangelists and mighty prophets, but poorly skilled leaders. We provide shallow, immature and positional leadership that have not made the church to truly fulfill her divine potentials in this part of the world. True, servant and healthy leadership have been the bane of the church here and that is what this book is out to address.

This book is primarily for young and up coming leaders who want to bring divine infusion into the leadership of the church. It is also for veteran leaders who desire to change and bring something new to the way they have been leading. Above all, every Christian should benefit from this book, because the young Christian of today will be the leader of tomorrow.

The tragedy had been that many people only start to learn leadership when they have gotten to a leadership position. The more reason they lead badly. A better way is to start learning leadership when you are still young, so that you can provide healthy leadership wherever you find yourself.

Like I noted earlier, many excellent resources on leadership abound. However, majority of them have dealt with the functions of a leader and the technical aspects of leadership, but this book will deal with the personal life of the leader. I'm of the strong opinion that if the leader is okay in his personal life, his leadership will become better. I believe that leadership is not found in a position but in a person.

Also, you cannot live wrong and lead right. So, the personal life and relational aspects of leadership are what this book will address squarely.

I'm convinced that your life and leadership will never be the same again. As you go through this book, allow the contents to go through you over and over again. Reading a book is never enough, your response to what you read matters much more.

Dr. Francis Bola Akin-John.
June 2008

Healthy Leaders, Healthy Churches

Pastoring or Leading The Church Today

"It is only the purest form of leadership that will work in the church"

It is not possible to manage or pastor a local church to durable growth. You can only lead the church to sustainable growth. The church is not a thing to be managed, but it consist of people to be led.

A church can be wonderfully pastored but poorly led. I know a church where the leader is a wonderful pastor. He is people-oriented and had a heart for God. He is a good shepherd and has unequalled integrity, but he is a poor leader. His leadership skills are very minimal compared to his pastoral abilities.

Well, the church he started 25 years ago with great promises from God had only grown to 20 branches with less than 2,000 congregants. With the caliber of people, teachings and promises from God that the church possessed, if she has grown to hundreds of thousands of members, it would have been a tip of the iceberg. But the church is a lame duck and unable to fulfill her great potentials simply because the founder is more of a pastor than a healthy leader of people.

This true story is found in every denomination and church affiliation today. Local churches can only thrive when healthy leaders are in control.

A pastor

A pastor is someone with a shepherd's heart. He is protective in nature and enjoys close-knit fellowship with people. A true pastor is a mother chicken that loves to protect the chicks and broods over them. A pastor teaches, tends, cares and visits the people and nurtures them. He loves to be in control and makes the people dependent on him.

A pastor finds it hard to delegate to others and he is usually threatened by the gift and grace in the lives of others. A good pastor develops his sheep – followers, and he loves to be seen as doing all the work. A typical example of this kind of pastor is Moses. He was the shepherd of a church in the wilderness. He pastored them very well, until he met father Jethro. Father Jethro taught him to move from the pastoring level to leadership mode (Exodus 18:13-26.)

With the kind insight and experience of father Jethro, Moses was able to shift from pastoring to leadership mode in the church. It was then the work took a turn for the better and he and the church were able to endure.

The work will not last as long as we remain in the pastoring level. We ourselves will not last. It needs to be stated clearly that you cannot pastor a church to real growth, you can only lead a church to sustainable growth. You can pastor until your church is 100 members but after that, you will have to become a leader. The shepherd in verse 1 of Psalm 23 later grew to lead the sheep in verse 2. Sheep must not only be shepherded but also well led. Leading them is much more beneficial, both to the sheep and the leader.

> *...you cannot pastor a church to real growth, you can only lead a church to sustainable growth.*

A healthy leader

In the church, the pastor must grow to become the leader. The Lord doesn't lead His church by committees, but by one man, ably supported by committees. Like every other human organization, leadership is very crucial to the health and well-being of the church. But much more than any other human organization, the church is the most leadership intensive entity on earth. *Because the church is the agent of divine transformation, her leadership must be of the purest and highest kind.*

More than any other time in history, the local church needs healthy leaders today. Healthy leadership is very complicated. It has many facets – it requires seasoning, learning, spirituality, relational skills, courage,

Healthy Leaders, Healthy Churches

experience, love, care, vision, empowerment and servant heart. A healthy leader is a growing leader. To be a growing leader is to be flexible, change-friendly, adaptable, excellence driven, in touch with God and seeking for improvement and impact in every area of life and ministry. A healthy leader is a kingdom-minded leader. He seeks God's kingdom more than anything else.

> *Healthy leaders will always lead to healthy churches and sick leaders will always lead to sick and diseased churches.*

A healthy leader brings God's power fully into the work. He is first and foremost a sound Christian with a burning heart for God and his motive of leading is to serve God and the people with the intention of expanding the frontiers of God's kingdom in the world.

The Pastor must grow to become a true leader in the church. People are not looking for perfect leaders, but growing ones. Stagnant, non-growing and incompetent leaders cannot lead the church up, but down. Healthy leaders will always lead to healthy churches and sick leaders will always lead to sick and diseased churches.

Purest form of leadership

There are many definitions of leadership, and many secular ideas of leadership have found their way into the church. As a spiritual entity, it is only leadership that thrives and is built solely on influence that will bring true

Healthy Leaders, Healthy Churches

progress to the church. Simply put, pure leadership in the church is influence. The ability to make people follow without force, coercion and manipulation. It is gaining respect with people that will make them to willingly follow you to accomplish a vision that will benefit God, humanity and themselves.

In other organizations, if all else fails, the leader can rely on his position to cow people into submission. But in the church, leaders only have their influence to aid them. This is so because positional leadership doesn't work much. If a leader doesn't have influence, he will simply become ineffective.

During the earthly ministry of our Lord Jesus, He did not specifically choose a leader for the disciples, until His resurrection appearance. He deliberately allowed the leader to emerge through influence. In John chapter 21, nine of the disciples followed Peter to fish, leaving only one person behind. But then they were eleven as a result of Judas's betrayal and suicide.

Having seen that Peter had gained much influence with the disciples which warranted their followership of him, Jesus wasted no time in appointing Peter as the official leader of the disciples. This is the pure leadership that can only work in the church. The leader must be the person with the most influence. True influence is when people follow you wholeheartedly without gimmick, threats, cunningness, craftiness and force.

Real influence is being the person others will gladly and confidently follow. Influence cannot be mandated, it must be earned. Influence doesn't come automatically, it is a process. When a leader has little influence, little

Healthy Leaders, Healthy Churches

can be achieved. And when a leader has much influence, much can be achieved. You can build or burst your influence by your actions and inactions.

Whenever a new leader comes to a church, or you start a new work or ministry, not everybody will accept or follow you and your idea. You must build relationships, grow your influence and demonstrate that you meant well. You will not be able to influence everyone at the same level or at the same time. While some may be skeptical of you, some will follow afar off, while others will follow haphazardly, few others will follow you body, soul and spirit.

Pure leadership in the church is trust. When people can trust you, then you can influence them. Trust is the emotional glue that binds leaders and followers together. If people cannot trust you, then you cannot influence them and they will not follow you. Healthy leaders consciously build trust and influence through integrity, love, character, care, personal growth, vision and generousity.

If people cannot trust you, then you cannot influence them and they will not follow you.

Our influence as leaders has little to do with our positions or title than it does with the life we live. It is not about position, it is about life. When leaders fail to remove barriers to influence in their lives then they cannot lead people well. The fact that you are a pastor or founder of a church doesn't mean people will follow your leadership. You will have to consciously build your influence and become the leader that can be trusted and followed. In the past, people easily believe and follow leaders. Not any more. You will have to earn the trust and believe of people today through your transparent, godly and dynamic leadership abilities.

How our churches are being led

It is most unfortunate that majority of our big and small churches are being led in the wrong ways today. In actual fact, church leaders in Africa have largely imbibed the secular leadership philosophy of the political leaders. Just as the political leaders grab power, hoard power and use it to oppress, dominate, subjugate and maltreat the people, the same way the leaders of our churches are doing. Just as the political leaders corner all the money and spend it on themselves and their cronies, the same way church leaders are doing. Just as the political leaders hate criticism and dissenting voices, so also our church leaders. Just as the political leaders use their position to enrich themselves at the detriment of the nation and people, so also some church leaders use the church to better their lot in life at the expense of the kingdom of God.

Just as the political leaders turn blind eye to corruption and stealing of public funds by their associates, much the same way church leaders sweep sins and evils being perpetrated by their associates under the carpet, because they themselves are not free from such vices. Any wonder why the church is lame-duck today and sincere people are losing faith in the church?

Healthy Leaders, Healthy Churches

Internal crisis, infighting, downward spiral and breakaways are so rife in churches today due to these unhealthy ways of leadership. Churches that seem good, big and wonderful far away, are rotten and crisis ridden at close quarters simply because of these unhealthy leadership practices. The fight for position, political and arm-twisting tactics that is rife in our secular leadership have also gained ground in the church. The more reason many local churches and denominations are struggling for survival today.

On the other hand, the numerical growth of churches without corresponding spiritual vitality has thrown up many carnal people into leadership positions. Today, we see people with the old nature of sin, immorality, jealousy, wickedness and injustice, leading spiritual entities. Small wonder that the church is not living up to expectation.

Development of leadership skill

Healthy churches call for leaders to develop their ability to lead. Prophets, evangelists, teachers, apostles, pastors and bishops must grow to become healthy leaders. Even if you are a called and born leader, you still need to develop your ability to lead very well. Low leadership ability has been the limit that brought limitation to so many promising churches and ministries.

One can be highly anointed and gifted, and yet, have very low ability to lead. For such people, the good news is that leadership can be learned and the skill can be sharpened.

Healthy Leaders, Healthy Churches

"So he fed them according to the integrity of his heart; and guided them by the skillfulness of his hands." (Psalm 78:72).

David was a man of integrity and skillful hands. He displayed a honest and sincere heart plus skillfulness of hands to lead the people.

Leading the church to progress and health demands that leaders must acquire, hone, sharpen and fine-tune their skills and ability to lead effectively.

Church leaders of today must have these two qualities in large measure. It is not enough to have a heart of integrity. There must also be skillful hands. In actual fact, if you have integrity but your leadership skill is poor or non-existent, then your work will always suffer. Leading the church to progress and health demands that leaders must acquire, hone, sharpen and fine-tune their skills and ability to lead effectively:

Now, allow me to summarize the kind of leadership that will bring health to the church today. These are ten truths about real church leadership:

1. **The church is the most leadership intensive organization in the world.**

It is only the purest and genuine kind of leadership that will work in the church. In the army, leadership is authoritarian. In the secular world, you either obey or

Healthy Leaders, Healthy Churches

you are sent packing. But in the church, it is not so, because the church is a free society.

No law binds people to the church. If they are not being well led, they move away to another church. So, true leadership must be on display, if sustainable growth will happen.

2. Leadership is not found in a position, but in a person.

Unfortunately, most people in leadership position in the church have not learned this truth. We award positions, title and ordination to people hoping to make them leaders. Today, there is crisis of true leadership in the church, not because there are vacancy in positions, but because real leaders are not leading. Position doesn't make a leader; it is the leader that makes the position.

3. Leadership determines the level of churches.

Of course, we all know that no church will rise higher than her leadership. Whether a church will become a small, medium size or large church will be determined by the kind and worth of leadership being provided. Whether a church will move forward to fulfill her destiny and impact the world or remain small, lame-duck and stagnant, will largely be determined by her leadership. No church has ever risen above her leadership.

4. Transformed churches start from transformed leaders.

If a church is going to be an agent of transformation

in the personal, family, business and spiritual lives of people, it usually starts from her leaders. If the leaders are carnal, sinful, ungodly and not transformed by God, the church also will be full of such people. The spiritual health of any church is tied to the spiritual health of her leaders.

The weaknesses of the leaders will be the weaknesses of the church. The revival of the church rests in the hand of her leaders. No church has the power to become anything in the absence of her leaders. You cannot give what you don't have. You cannot lead better than who you are.

5. Leadership is influence in the church.

It is not position, title, age, wealth, anointing, status and connection. It is a divine call, coupled with the skillful ability to rally people to a common cause. It is the ability to make people follow you without coercing and subjugating them. It is people seeing something in you that is not in them and therefore decide to follow you.

Influence comes in various leadership stages and it takes time to build. Without influence, even if you are speaking the truth, like Joshua, people will still not follow you. Infact, people will stone you for speaking the truth, if you have little or no influence.

6. Purpose, direction and result hold the key.

Healthy church leadership is providing purpose and direction to the people. People want to follow someone who has proven to know the way. Purposeful direction coupled with tangible results are the keys to leadership

Healthy Leaders, Healthy Churches

in the church. Leading for results and production will elicit the confidence of the people. The people must be able to point to tangible things that have happened and are still happening to them under your leadership. Without such results, there will be no respect. People always follow someone who shows result.

7. People are the greatest asset of true leadership.

Healthy church leadership is not self-benefit, but for the benefit of people. The people must be loved, served, helped, assisted, trained and empowered to succeed in God and in the world. People are the real reason for leading. Without the ability to motivate, communicate, relate and enable people, true leadership will still be wanting. Healthy church leadership is not being lords over God's people – subjugating, using and dumping them according to your whims and caprices. Rather, it is empowering, equipping and enabling God's people to be all that God creates them to be.

8. Trust is the glue that binds leaders and followers together.

In the secular world, people can tolerate the leaders they don't trust, but not in the church. They will either follow you or leave your church. Actually, people don't really leave churches, they only leave their leaders. When church leaders display integrity, transparency, honesty and sincerity, people trust and follow them whole-heartedly.

But when the reverse is the case, people forsake their leaders en masse. Church leaders today must work to earn the trust of the people due to past ungodly examples that have done much damage to the image of ministers. If people cannot trust you as a leader, then you cannot be followed.

9. Team building brings effectiveness

Lone ranger leaders who run solo ministries are always a minus for the church. Healthy church leadership calls for team work. It doesn't have to be lonely at the top. The leader must choose his team and train them to work together. He must be the leader among his team mates. The team must support and help him to succeed. Patriarchs and Matriarchs in the church must submit to him. Associates must be loyal and compliment his efforts. Team work always makes the dream work.

10. No vacuum in leadership: It's either up or down.

The progress, growth and dynamism of any church still answers to leadership. The church will go up or move down based on the type of people in leadership positions. There is no middle ground: it is either you lead the church up or you lead her down. Leaders that are afraid of change and taking decisions will surely destroy the church, even if they are godly people. When church leaders want peace at all cost and remain ultra-conservative, they will lead the church down.

In conclusion, leadership is so crucial to God that He sometimes tolerate weak and bad leaders rather than no leaders at all. God depends on leaders to carry on His work. God calls leaders to step forward and lead revolution for Him. If you want to be a leader after the heart of God, then you must seek to be a healthy one.

Healthy Leaders, Healthy Churches

God is desperately searching for healthy leaders to bring revival, divine power and spiritual depth to His churches all over the world. If you are an unhealthy leader and God has been tolerating you so far, He will not tolerate you forever. Today is the time to change and imbibe the traits that will make you healthy leaders so that you can count in the estimate of God.

TAKE HOME

Ponder on these questions to improve yourself.

1. How have you been handling the church? Pastoring or Leading?

2. Can you spot the differences between a Pastor and a Leader?

3. Are you a positional or an influential leader?

4. How has your leadership determine the level of your church?

5. Are you a healthy or a sick leader?

NOTE

If you have been found wanting in any area of your leadership, start working on yourself now!

The Rise And Fall Of Churches

"More than anybody else, leaders have the power to kill churches."

A certain preacher came to the limelight about 15 years ago. He started a church in Lagos and was very fervent in prayers. In no time the church grew and local branches sprang up here and there. Large prayer conferences were being organized in stadium with thousands of people in attendance. Many wealthy people were attracted to the preacher and he had the ears of the well-to-do and mighty in the society. He moved in convoys of cars and buses to towns and cities across Nigeria. The anointing was working and miracles were happening. But poor leadership skills were in display by the preacher.

After some few years, the church started going down due to uncontrollable spending of the leader. His moral lapses came to the open and the leader had to bolt away when the heat became too unbearable. Today, almost all those local branches have closed down and the preacher is struggling to revive a once promising ministry.

> *The health and durability of any church is hinged on the durability quality of her leaders.*

This is one out of the numerous true life stories of preachers, both conservative and charismatic, whose ministries have suffered a shipwreck due to low ability to lead. There is always a very strong correlation between a church and her leaders. The health and durability of any church is hinged on the durability quality of her leaders.

Life cycle of churches

Over the years, I've always taught the life cycle of churches in many of our seminars and conferences. The life cycle of a church is almost always like the human life cycle, but with a little difference. Now, let's look at it stage by stage.

Stage 1: The birth

Local churches are birthed through God's call upon a man or a denomination plants a daughter church and appoints a pastor to head the church. For a new church to be healthy, the pastor must be allowed to lead and given the free hand to operate and initiate programmes that will help the sure footing of the church. The members must be well taught, assimilated and built up in the Lord. A new church doesn't start growing immediately, it usually takes some time – a year, two or more. The foundation of a church will affect her growth and health.

Stage 2: The growth

Growth is the end result of doing something right. Naturally, growth should not be a problem in the church if everything is being done biblically. Churches start to grow numerically, spiritually, materially and financially from their second year upward. The growth might be triggered by spiritual factors such as fasting, prayers, miracles, healings, deliverance and mighty display of the gifts of the spirit.

The church will grow for 2, 5, 7, 10 years without any serious crisis or breakaway. In many cases, from 10 years upward, the church will generally start having internal tensions and muted dissensions due to perceived leadership weaknesses. If these weaknesses are not addressed, the church will get to plateau stage and stop there.

Stage 3: The plateau

At this stage, the church will start experiencing a kind of balanced exodus. Which means that while some people are moving away, other people are coming in. If two people moved away due to problems noticed in the leadership, one new person will come and join the church and the leadership will think that everything is still okay. To them, 'It is only the disgruntled elements that are moving away'. The truth however is that the church is no longer growing but only maintaining those who are inside. The church has started losing steam gradually, but only the trained eye could see it at this stage. Unfortunately, the church can remain at this state for the next 7 to 10 years, before the bubble will burst.

Stage 4: The decline

By the time the church moves to this stage, the downward spiral has started in earnest. At decline stage, the church will start to experience breakaway and massive losses. Members will move away in groups, families and whole local branches will follow suit. Much more people will be going away than those who are coming in. The church is bleeding seriously and those who are the future of the church are either moving to another church or they are starting their own churches. It is at this stage that many leaders admit the truth they have denied for years.

Unfortunately, the leaders that brought the church to this unenviable stage still sit tight and refused to leave

Healthy Leaders, Healthy Churches

the stage for younger leaders, claiming that 'it is my church and I started it with my sweat and blood'. Well, the church has no choice than to move to the next and final stage.

Stage 5: The death

Since the church had bled for years, the normal thing is death. Too many churches have died and are dying today due to wrong leadership practises. Sometimes, churches die by closing down and being sold to other churches. I've seen churches that literally closed down after years of near-empty worship services, and these were once thriving churches, brimming with enthusiastic worshippers! The numbers of such churches are increasing daily due to problematic and unhealthy leaders.

It needs to be stated clearly that the only hope for a church not to come to stage four and five is healthy leadership. A growing church needs healthy leaders to keep growing and a plateaued church equally needs healthy leaders for renewal and upward movement. So long a church is lacking healthy leaders, her decline and death will come in earnest. Leaders that led a church to decline cannot lead her up. They have lost the credibility to bring turn around to the church. They will have to humble themselves and seek for godly and dynamic successors to replace them; else the church will continue to flounder under them until she will get to the stage of retrogression and death.

The only other option for such leaders is that they should take time off to learn, relearn and unlearn many of the prejudices and notions that have contributed greatly to their downward journey. They should take a course in healthy leadership, church growth, church health and transformation. Peradventure, that will help them to bring turn around to the church, provided they still have the heart to take hard and courageous decisions for growth and progress.

What brings people and what keeps them

Healthy leaders must realize that what brings people to church is different to what keeps them. Many church leaders have those things that bring people such as power demonstration, prophetic pronouncements, anointing, miracles, signs and wonders, prayer ministry and deliverance, but they lack those things that keep people in the church. What keeps people are leadership skills, proper administration, sound and balanced teachings, relational skills and inner resources.

Many preachers have spent all their time and life focusing only on what brings people to church and failed abysmally to balance it with what keeps people. The more reason their churches enter plateau, decline and retrogression stages quickly. I'm aware of churches that grow for sometime, but started declining because the leaders have little regard for those factors that keep

Healthy leaders must realize that what brings people to church is different to what keeps them.

Healthy Leaders, Healthy Churches

and nurture people in the church.

How leaders instalmentally kill churches

To instalmentally or progressively kill a church means to lead a church to downward spiral; to jeopardize the growth and future potentials of a church; to turn a spiritually strong church to a carnal, worldly and social institution. To cause quarrel, animosity, bickering, chaos, internal wranglings that debar a church from focusing on the right thing; to allow sin, evil and corruption to reign unchecked in the church until majority is defiled. To bring strange fire, doctrine and practices that drives out the true presence and power of God in the church.

A dying church is once a strong, durable, dynamic, vibrant and growing church but is now near empty, stagnant, declining, dogmatic and lifeless.

Quite sadly, there are pastors and leaders who are experts in killing churches. They have certificates from the devil's school of destruction to bring death and decay to living churches. One of such men was taken to a young church with over 100 members, but after twelve years of pastoring them, he led them down to less than 30 members. I know another pastor that always bring backwardness, stagnation and woes to any church he is transferred to. If they are growing before his arrival, they will stop growing, physically, materially, financially and numerically after his arrival. The church will only start growing again the day he is taken away!

Healthy Leaders, Healthy Churches

Usually, churches don't die immediately or instantaneously, rather they die gradually, progressively and instalmentally. Allow me to enumerate how General Overseers, Pastors and Associate Pastors kill churches instalmentally.

a) General Overseers' role in killing churches

* Living in secret sins and ungodliness
* Employing and ordaining any kind of pastor to lead the churches
* Lack of improvement and increase in the capacity to lead.
* Ordaining but don't train or monitor pastors under them.
* Loving and placing deacons and elders above the pastors.
* Employing wrong administration and arm-twisting tactics to lead.
* Controlling, guarding and directing from the bedroom.
* Not allowing the branches the freedom to initiate and grow.
* Turning the local branches to supermarkets and collecting all their monies.
* Being petty, jealous and envious at the gifts and graces of the under-leaders.
* Having no clear goal, vision, focus and direction for the church.
* Refusing to learn, change and grow.
* Being the all in all and accountable to no one.
* Building the church on yourself and your gifts alone.
* Teaching only one line of truth and refusing to balance it.
* Letting your wife and family be in control of the

Healthy Leaders, Healthy Churches

    finances.
* Not planning, praying and preparing for a better future for the work.
* Driving away genuine associates and surround yourself with yes men and bootlickers.
* Not correcting any perceived error but glossing over them.

b) Pastors' role in killing churches

* Being a nominal, carnal and ungodly pastor
* Being involved in secret, moral and financial scams
* Not building on Christ and the word of God, but on yourself
* Being prayerless and not praying for the church – Being too busy
* Allowing sin to rule and reign in the church – God understands
* Don't discipline those who did evil – it will offend them
* Don't expose them to the whole counsel of God – they will run away
* Don't live what you preach – God understands your weakness
* Encouraging division, suspicion and bickering among the people
* Being a politician – trickish, wayward, cunning and crafty
* Being highly prejudiced against learning, growing and change
* Being a weak and yo-yo leader that every one controls
* Being covetous of money, gain, profit and success only
* Always preaching on ephemeral things only, but not

teaching
* Having a demonized wife and ungodly children
* Don't take decisions that will help growth and progress
* Being a 'peace at all cost' man and mortgaging progress at the altar of peace
* Inviting a sinful, immoral, error-teaching and money making guest ministers

c) **Deacons, Elders, Boards and Associates' role in killing churches.**

* Not giving the pastor the free hand to lead the church.
* Spreading lies and rumor about the pastor
* Being bad examples and models
* Displaying disloyalty, disobedience and fight the pastor openly
* Finding fault with everyone and discovering mistakes in every decision
* Don't pay your tithes and offerings and discourage those who do.
* Don't show any commitment and when you see those who do, criticize them severely
* Though you are an under-leader, behave as your own boss
* Don't give opinion when asked, but later tell everyone how things should have been done
* Sowing seed of discord and lies among the brethren
* Don't bother to evangelize new people and drive away those who newly came by your actions and words.
* Always do secret meetings in members' houses with the topic: "*how to deal with the pastor*"
* Keep your eyes open for something wrong and

when you find it, spread it everywhere and threaten to quit the church.
* Don't support any change that will bring growth — because it is against church tradition
* Don't take time to pray, fast and intercede for the church and the pastor
* Always compare your church with the other churches
* Always support those who do evil and plan rebellion with them.

> *It must however be noted that those who partake in killing the church of Christ will never go scot-free.*

Many churches have been progressively killed and are still being killed as a result of these actions and inactions on the part of General Overseers, Pastors and Associate Leaders. Rather than abate, the number of such churches are on the increase today.

It must however be noted that those who partake in killing the church of Christ will never go scot-free. God will deal with them and avenge Himself. The church is the only property of God on earth and those leaders who contribute one way or the other into bringing death to the local body of believers will receive fiery judgment from the Lord unless they repent.

Apostle Paul wrote to young Timothy, **"But if I tarry long, that thou mayest know how thou oughtest to behave thyself in the house of God, which is the church of the living God, the pillar and ground of truth."** (I Timothy 3:15)

Healthy Leaders, Healthy Churches

Now, there are right and wrong ways to behave and handle the church of the living God. So long the name of Christ, the word of God and the Spirit of God are invoked upon a congregation, it is the church of the Living God. It doesn't belong to any man and God will not take it kindly if we behave wrongly and that assembly of saints has to enter a tailspin and die.

Those who made it a trademark to scatter and kill churches will always experience closed heaven over their lives; God's wrath and judgment; lack of favor, struggling, loss of heaven and reward. Heaven is sad, angels are downcast and Jesus is unhappy whenever a church is killed and incapacitated for kingdom expansion.

Let me close this chapter in an upbeat note by pinpointing what healthy leaders must be. These are qualities and traits that must be ingrained deeply into the root and fabric of the life of a spiritually healthy church leader:

Leaders are **Dealers** in hope – they inspire hope in others

Leaders are **Readers** – they study to improve their skills

Leaders are **Seers** – they see more and deeper than others

Leaders are **Intuitive** – they read situations very well

Leaders are **Learners** – the more they learn, t h e

Healthy Leaders, Healthy Churches

better they lead

Leaders are **Thinkers** – they think big, deep and high

Leaders are **Trustworthy** – they know that is their solid ground

Leaders are **Lifters** – they don't limit but lift others

Leaders are **Equippers** – they invest in others to succeed

Leaders are **Listeners** – they listen to God and the people

Leaders are **Communicators** – they speak clearly, simply and consistently

Leaders are **Initiators** – they create and initiate new ways

Leaders are **Planners** – they chart the course and set the target

Leaders are **Loving** – they don't keep a score but forgive

Leaders are **Ladders** – they allow others to climb up

Leaders are **Servants** – they are service and power oriented

Leaders are **Magnetic** – they attract and hold

followers

Leaders are **Focused** – they have intensity and concentration

Leaders have **Prayer life** – the authority to lead is found in the ability to pray

Leaders have **Right attitudes** – your attitude is always your choice

Leaders are **Decisive** – they are not afraid to take decisions

Leaders are **Courageous** – they take calculated risks.

TAKE HOME

Ponder on these questions to improve yourself.

1. What stage is your church now?

2. Do you have what brings people to church?

3. Do you have what keeps people in the church?

4. If your chruch has gottento plateau or decline stage, how do you intend to revamp the situation?

5. Have you contributed in anyway to killing the church, if yes, how do you intend to repent and restitute?

NOTE

If you don't begin the process of reversing the negative condition of that church now, when are you going to start?

Healthy Leaders, Healthy Churches

Chapter Two

The Rise And Fall of Churches

Weaknesses of Leaders that Weaken Churches

"People don't really leave churches, they only leave leaders because of their weaknesses."

It is worth reiterating that leadership has much to do with a person than with position. The person and personality of a leader will give vent and direction to his leadership more than anything else. It is in the light of this that I want to examine the weaknesses of leaders that usually weaken churches and ministries.

Though, in Africa, we deify leaders and see them as gurus and small gods who cannot do any wrong and leaders revel and gloat on this, yet the truth is that leaders have weaknesses that usually weaken their leadership and work, if not properly addressed.

We can learn invaluable lessons that will help our overall leadership by the pinpointing of those weaknesses that can bring ruin and destruction to our ministries. Take Moses for an example. He felt weary of the complaining, murmuring, pettiness and critical spirit of the people (Numbers 20:1-12). Their rebellion got to him and he became angry at them. Directed by God to speak to a rock in order to get water for the people, but in anger he struck the rock. He reacted in fury rather than obeying with poise.

> *The person and personality of a leader will give vent and direction to his leadership more than anything else.*

And for this disobedience – in moment of weakness, he was barred from entering the promised land! His weakness? He reacted when he should have been proactive.

Today, many leaders are reacting to people and situations and they are losing their ministries and reward. Sometimes, weaknesses are not outright sins, but shortcomings in our character and personalities that need to be addressed. At other times, they are sins that want to jeopardize the life of God within us and our ministries.

In biblical examples, Samson had a weakness for women and because it was not addressed, it eventually ruined him. Prophet Ballam had a weakness for money – and he sold his anointing for some couple of coins and lost his life. King Saul had fear as his weakness and that fear made him to disobey God to please the people and he lost his kingdom.

Healthy Leaders, Healthy Churches

"Take us the foxes, the little foxes that spoil the vines: for our vines have tender grapes." (Song of Solomon 2:15)

Because leaders stand in front of people, their mistakes and weaknesses are much more pronounced than others. The personal and leadership weakness of a leader, no matter how little they are, will be open for all to see and if not urgently addressed, they will weaken the work. Some leaders thought that their weaknesses and private inadequacies will not have any effect on the work. How wrong they are! The private and personal weaknesses, mistakes and sins of leaders will always have terrific and telling effect on the work. Since leadership doesn't operate in a vacuum and it's not an abstract thing, but embodied in a person, the weaknesses of the leader will always be the weakness of the church.

"Your glorying is not good. Know ye not that a little leaven leaveneth the whole lump?" (I Cor. 5:6).

Let's see some of the weaknesses that weaken churches: **"For the leaders of this people cause them to err, and they that are led of them are destroyed."** (Isaiah 9:16)

1. Having one ear only:

Naturally, we are created to have two ears — meaning that we must hear from both sides, but I have seen many church leaders who only have one ear! They hear from one side and pass judgment immediately. This is a great weakness in many leaders in Nigeria and Africa.

Healthy Leaders, Healthy Churches

A church started a new local branch in Lagos, Nigeria and they went and got a pastor to help them lead the church. The pastor did well and by the second year, attendance had jumped to over 1,000 people. Few years later, the Overseer came and relieved him of his pastoral duties, saying that the Holy Ghost would want him to leave. But the truth is that some members of the church had fed the Overseer with lies. He later regretted his actions, but the pastor had left to start another great work.

I know of leaders that disciplined and sent their pastors packing as a result of anonymous letters or petition from members. They will never bother to cross-check facts with their pastors, neither will they give them opportunity to defend themselves. As a result of this weak leadership trait, they have lost many of their committed and foundational leaders that could have helped to lead the church to greater dimension of God.

Unfortunately, this weakness is so strong in some leaders that they are not even on speaking terms with those who have left their ministries. They usually regard them as 'backsliders' and 'false prophets'. Many churches had been greatly weakened due to this unwholesome practice. Today, these churches are on the down ward swing. What a shame!

2. Threat of multi-talented and shinning Associates:

Just as king Saul was greatly threatened with the shining of young David and plotted to kill him several times, so also many leaders are still displaying this

Healthy Leaders, Healthy Churches

weakness in large measure today. I know of a church where the leader doesn't want any other minister to pray for people, and he actually stopped those who pray for people with attendant miracles from doing so. He is unhappy when his associates are being appreciated for the gifts of God in their lives. He usually transfer such associates to far away places. He stops them from writing books and if anyone does, his name must appear as the author!

In other churches, multi-talented associates are castigated, rubbished publicly and condemned during the preaching sessions so as to diminish their rising status, and every political and carnal gimmick will be used until they will leave the church. This is the main reason for breakaways and large number of people leaving denominational churches to start their own independent ministries. Unfortunately, they too display this weakness after some time. Talk of 'evil carry over'!

Insecurity makes leaders to do stupid and foolish things. Insecure leaders are dangerous to themselves, their followers and the ministry or church they lead. Insecure leaders don't like others. They take more from people than they give. They continually limit their people and they permanently limit their church and ministry. Insecure leaders will always sabotage their leadership. Once you feel insecure, fear will eventually cause you to undermine your leadership. Genuine and healthy leaders must feel secure

> *Insecure leaders are dangerous to themselves, their followers and the ministry or church they lead.*

Healthy Leaders, Healthy Churches

when people stop liking them, when funding drops, when moral dips, when trouble comes or when others reject them.

3. Playing safe and afraid to offend:

Church leaders who are afraid to stick out their neck have this weakness in large measure. They are afraid to offend people and they keep quiet on salient issues they should speak clearly and urgently on, hoping that the issue will go away and die a natural death. I know of leaders who keep silent when it is discovered that under-leaders are found in sin, drunkenness, immorality and doctrinal error. They are too considerate of the feelings of the offender and in the effort to maintain peace, decide that silence is the best approach. Well, such leaders have unwittingly promoted rebellion, sinfulness and double standard in the church and among the people.

Many times, silence is golden, but in these times, silence is criminal. Pursuing peace at-all-cost as a leader will jeopardize progress in the church. Leaders that always sacrifice peace at the altar of progress will bring ruin and destruction to the work. In countless churches and ministries, this weakness have signalled the beginning of the end for many promising work of God

4. Suspicion and lack of trust:

I know a church leader that doesn't trust any of his staff, workers and associate leaders. Though he trained and equipped them, yet he is suspicious of them and will send spies to monitor their activities. Though he delegates work to them, yet he will not allow them to do it and he is constantly watching over their shoulders. I usually refer to the church as "KGB secret service" church. Everyone is trained to spy on his or her brother and make a report – whether true or trump up and the leader usually act on such reports to the detriment of his leadership and church. This is a widespread weakness of leaders that has helped to sabotage churches.

Leaders that suspect and fail to trust others as a result of past nasty experience with associates will always short change themselves and their ministries.

Leaders that suspect and fail to trust others as a result of past nasty experience with associates will always short change themselves and their ministries. Such leaders are playing God. If God can forgive us and trust us despite all our failings and disappointments, who are we not to trust others? If God had held on to our past records, He would have nobody to carry on His work in the world.

5. Use and dump them syndrome:

This is another great weakness that is very rife in the life and leadership of many church leaders in our Nation and Continent. Associates, ministers and missionaries are being used and yet there is no care for them. They are made to give 120% commitment to the vision of the leader, yet they could not be empowered to fulfill their own personal and family vision. When they are healthy, agile and productive, the church uses them but when they are sick, weak and incapacitated somehow, the leader forgets them and dumps them.

The wages and salaries that many leaders pay to their workforce is also appalling. While the leaders live in wealth and splendor, the workers live in abject poverty, penury and deprivation. Most of such leaders operate with the mindset that "I have suffered before I got to where I am now. So, let others suffer too". Well, these workers are the ones that did the bulk of the work that got you to where you are today and caring for them and paying them living wages is the sane thing to do.

Elisha was a leader that had this weakness too. The records that we had about his workers were not encouraging. One of the sons of the prophet died without paying his debt (2 Kings 4:1-7) and Gehazi was cursed severely, even to his generations, simply because he took the gifts, that apparently Elisha had failed to give to them and rejected again when someone else brought it to them!

While not excusing the despicable behaviour of Gehazi, one wonder why the prophet cursed him to his generations? Cursing him alone is bad, but to add his generations is very bad for a leader of the status of Elisha. That is why he had nobody to bury him when he died and he was buried in a shallow grave and his bones were open for all to see!

Church leaders that punish and deprive their staff good pay, care and physical nurturing, will always mortgage their future and that of their work.

Healthy Leaders, Healthy Churches

6. Unjust anger:

This is another major weakness of leaders. Leaders take decisions and act out of anger, bitterness and furious hearts. Moses was a classic example here. He got angry and instead of speaking, he smote the rock the second time, thereby destroying the typology of Christ.

Too many church leaders get angry over petty and little things and allow their anger to make them destroy what they had laboured for years to build. Hot temprament had been the major minus of leaders. Leaders have castigated, condemned and cursed their people under the influence of anger and annoyance.

"For the wrath of man worketh not the righteousness of God" (James 1:20).

Indeed and in truth, anger had destroyed many works of God. A pastor got angry and threw a bunch of keys at a sleeping member. the keys punched a hole in the head and blood gushed out and the member beat the pastor to a plump. What a shame! Senior pastors have acted in wrath and thereby sacked, transfered, purnished and sent away their associates, which they later regretted.

> *Too many church leaders get angry over petty and little things and allow their anger to make them destroy what they had laboured for years to build.*

Taking decisions in rage and acting when you are

under the influence of wrath will always sabotage your leadership. You will have to work seriously to overcome this deficit in your life, if you hope to be a healthy leader.

7. Money at all cost attitude:

Judas was a leader that displayed this weakness in his life and it ruined him. He sold his Lord for thirty pieces of silver because he could not overcome his weakness for money. He wants it at all cost, even if he had to sell his Lord! Prophet Ballam is also another leader that could not overcome his weakness for money. Even when God instructed him not to follow Balak, he still went ahead, because he could not resist the pay. He therefore lost his God and eventually his life. He died with the enemies of God.

I'm aware of many leaders today, who display this weakness in their churches and ministries. They can be your friend in everything, except in the area of money. They are ready to cut-corners and use any means to gain much more money. They water down the truth of the gospel; speak what people want to hear so that they can gain more money.

A certain Pastor sold his church at Ibadan to another church due to poor attendance and bad image in the community. The new Pastor declared that the Lord told him that the church hall was a citadel of Satan. When they were about to possess the property, they took time to do warfare prayers and started digging. Behold, they found many charms, occultic paraphernalia and panoply in the church compound. Why is this so? Because the former Pastor wanted to make money at all cost, he had to resort to using devilishand occultic powers to draw crowds and hoodwink them of their monies. If you think this is an isolated case, then you must be mistaken. Preachers are selling their anointing, soul and conscience just to make money in the ministry.

Preachers do many evil things, engage in unethical business practises, turn the ministry into money making ventures and sprinkle everything with the name of Jesus and some abstract scriptural passages to deceive and delude the heart of the simple.

The weakness of money at all cost have made leaders to receive donations from known crooks, frolic with thieving State Governors and give church positions to the highest bidder. It has also made General Overseers and Bishops to personalize all money in the church and turn the ministry of our Lord into personal financial empire. This weakness always cut short the life of any leader and the work they represent. It has brought ruin to many of them and is still ruining them.

8. Abusive tendencies:

It is common to think we should keep mum over the abuses that are going on in many church circles, believing that being critical of other Christian leaders is not biblical. But the truth is that these abuses are common and widespread, and someone will need to speak out. We can summarize every other leadership weakness under this heading.

Abusive leaders are strong-willed, power-seeking, power-hungry, control-oriented, self-centered, despots, tyrants and authoritarian rulers who masquerade as leaders. They use guilt, fear, dread and intimidation to manipulate and control members. They inflict spiritual, emotional, financial, mental, family and psychological violence on their people. Abusive leaders behave as lords over God's heritage. Abusive leaders violate the trust of the people, abuse their authority and use ecclesiastical power to control, manipulate, dominate, subordinate and subjugate the flock. Many of these leaders claim fundamental theology and are evangelical.

It is a reality that abuses do take place in the context of doctrinally sound, bible-preaching, fundamental and conservative Christianity. Abusive leaders and churches often start with noble intentions and biblical aspirations, but were led astray through human frailties. Whenever a leader is accountable to no one and therefore beyond confrontation, abuses will occur. Some example will suffice:

A certain church leader used gimmickry to fleece people of their money. He manipulated the scripture for motivational talks and demanded blind loyalty from the people. He used the emblem of candles and feet washing to razzmatazz people, but he will not bury them nor marry them.

Another leader encouraged the people to live as a community and the church owned all the property and took over the material possessions of the people. Yet another church leader used vision, dreams and prophecies to cow his members into submission and took over their wives, daughters, houses and finances in the name of the 'Lord'.

Another leader used preaching to isolate his people

and condemned every other church as evil. He even believed that every other church will close down to join his church and the people are made to work long hours with little or no pay. Small wonder many of them make a living by misappropriating the income of the church.

Abusive leaders show these traits:
- Run a one man show
- See themselves as special and untouchable
- Foster rigidity and legalism
- Demand blind loyalty
- Unfeeling, uncaring and hard hearted
- Discourage questions
- Use divide and rule tactics
- Highlight spiritual experiences more than the scripture
- Feel insecure and threatened by gifted members
- Tele-guide and manipulate members' lives
- Use worldly wisdom to control the church
- Isolationism policy and closed to the public
- Personal interpretation of scripture as right
- Make leaving the church by members very painful
- Cruel to those who dare leave the church

The end result of these leadership abuses is that many lives have been ruined, marriage destroyed and faith in God damaged irreparably. Thousands of Christians do not attend any church on a given Sunday today, due primarily to the abuses they have suffered in their former churches.

Leaders that have discovered that they have abusive tendencies through the reading of this chapter must pray and work for change. If you have discovered any of these weaknesses in yourself and in your leadership, then you must start addressing them squarely. It is not a crime to have weaknesses, but it is a great crime not to address them. Don't let your weakness weaken you and your great ministry. Work over your weaknesses every day. Learn, grow, improve, change and strengthen yourself against those weaknesses that want to rubbish you and your work.

What people want to see In their leaders

It is fitting to end this chapter with the list of those qualities that people want to see in their leaders. Followers don't just want any type of leaders. There are qualities that they desire to see in their leaders. True leaders must work over their weaknesses and inculcate these qualities into their lives and leadership. Followers want to see:

1. **Calling** - Your calling from God must be clear and definite.

2. **Character** - Your character is the backbone of your leadership.

3. **Constraints** - You must remove all personal constraints and weaknesses in your life.

4. **Commitment** - Show commitment to God, His vision, people and kingdom.

5. **Conviction** - Have a strong conviction. Stand for what is right.

Healthy Leaders, Healthy Churches

6. **Change** - Learn to change, grow, improve and develop yourself.

7. **Charisma** - Have a magnet in your life that attracts others.

8. **Competence** - Show competency in the way things are being handled.

9. **Credibility** - Your credibility will always speak for you.

10. **Connection** - Be connected to God, His word and people.

11. **Courageous** - Show courage as a leader. Courage and cowardice are contagious.

12. **Christ centered** - Focus on Christ, live and seek His glory in all you do.

13. **Coach** - Be a coach to others and allow yourself to be coached.

14. **Crucifixion** - Crucify the flesh and live a disciplined life.

15. **Creativity** - Be innovative and creative in approach and problem handling.

16. **Consistency** - Dilly-dallying and inconsistency in life and messages put people off.

17. **Communication** - Be a communicator, not only a speaker.

True leaders must work these characteristics into their lives. It is then they can lead in a healthy and dynamic way. Healthy leaders must display these traits for followers to see in large measure, it is then they can lead the church up and not down.

"In reading the lives of great men, I found that the first victory they won was over themselves". - Harry S. Truman.

TAKE HOME

Ponder on these questions to improve yourself.

1. What are your own weaknesses? List them out.

2. How do you intend to work over these weaknesses so that they don't weaken your leadership?

3. As a leader, do you possess any of the traits or characteristics of an abusive leader? If yes, repent and restitute now!

4. How do you intend to inculcate those things people wants to see in their leaders into your own life?

Secret of Healthy Leadership: Lead Yourself First

"You are the greatest crowd you will ever lead."

True and healthy leadership starts from you and who you are. The power behind your leadership is the life you are living. Your life will always be your leadership. True leadership is more of who you are than what you do or accomplish.

A certain Emperor of a kingdom was walking at the outskirts of a city when he encountered a very old man walking ramrod straight in the opposite direction. *"Who are you?"* The emperor asked his subject. *"I am a king,"* replied the old man. *"A king?" "Over what kingdom do you reign?" "Over myself"*, was the proud old man's reply. Yes each of us is a monarch of our own lives. We are responsible for ruling our actions and decisions.

Greatest challenge

The greatest challenge any leader will face is that of leading himself well. The toughest person to lead is always you. It is always easy to control and teach others what to do, but to carry out such instruction by you is not easy. Many times, we look at leaders very far away and we think that everything is okay with them. But the truth is that they are all struggling with themselves. The toughest assignment of a leader is to himself. The greatest enemy of a leader is within himself. If you are able to lead yourself well always, then you can be your greatest asset, if not, you will be your own greatest liability.

Whether we are looking at biblical examples such as Noah, Abraham, Moses, Joseph, David, Samson, Peter and Paul, the reality is always the same. If you cannot lead yourself well, then you will fail in leading others.

The greatest challenge any leader will face is that of leading himself well.

"When we are foolish, we want to conquer the world. When we are wise, we want to conquer ourselves." – John Foster.

"*The only conquests which are permanent and leave no regrets are conquests of us. Don't try to conquer the world until you've taken care of things in your own backyard.*" – Napoleon.

The smallest crowd you will ever lead is you; but it's the most important one. If you do that well, then you will earn the right to lead bigger crowds. But if you don't lead yourself well, even if you get to lead crowds, then you'll make a mess of yourself and the people.

Leadership starts from you and yourself alone. If you don't lead yourself, you cannot lead others successfully. Healthy leaders lead themselves in the areas of spirituality, character, emotion, attitude, family and relationships.

a. Spirituality

To be religious is not to be spiritual. Rather, it is to have a vital and ongoing relationship with God through His son, Jesus Christ. It is to have the life of God within you, to be alive and set free from the chains and shackles of sins. That is the starting point of your spirituality. But then, you must start growing in the Lord. You cannot lead very well, if you have been disconnected from God. You must daily pray, read the scriptures, be filled with the Spirit of God and live by Christian virtues. If you have lost steam with God, then your leadership will suffer.

A leader in touch with God will have a tender and kind word for those he is leading and a leader out of touch with God will have a hard heart and harsh words. What you do everyday to deepen your walk with God is what will prove your ability to lead yourself and others very well.

b. Character

Your character is who you are. Reputation is what people know you for, but character is who you really are.

Healthy Leaders, Healthy Churches

It is what you do when nobody is watching. Self discipline, good values, integrity and clear sense of identity will help you to develop good and godly character. Weak character leads to compromise, wickedness, allowing evil, favoritism, petty jealousy and doing things for gain.

A strong and godly character will enable you to have good values, do what is right, operate by faith, believe what is good and be self-motivated. Your character base must be good and strong in order to provide good leadership. If you are vacillating, indecisive, men-pleasing and favour-seeking, you will always be a bad leader.

c. Emotion

You must be in control of your emotions. If you are given to fits of temper, you cannot really lead. If you are always moody, morose and downcast, you'll lose leadership. Short tempers don't make for good leadership. The inability to lead yourself very well in the area of your feelings will make you slave of your emotions.

Right emotional response in moment of crisis will assist you to rightly manage conflicts. If your personal life is based on feelings and people don't know what to expect from

> *A strong and godly character will enable you to have good values, do what is right, operate by faith, believe what is good and be self-motivated.*

you because they are not sure of your emotional state, then your leadership will lose respect. When your emotional ways get the better of you, then you are not leading yourself very well.

d. Attitude

The development of a positive attitude is the first conscious step towards becoming a healthy leader. Successful leadership cannot be constructed without this crucial building block. Your attitude is always your choice, no matter what happens to you. Your attitude is your behaviours, conduct, manners and comportment. It can be positive or negative.

Your attitude is truly the librarian of your past, speaker of your present and prophet of your future. Your attitude can help or hinder you; your attitude determines your approach to life and your relationship with people. Your attitude can turn problems into blessings and your attitude is not automatically good just because you are a Christian. You'll have to work on it and lead yourself very well here. You'll have to teach your heart love, care, forgiveness, forbearance and imbibe the ability to look at the positive side of life.

Your negative, critical, sarcastic, touchy, irritating attitudes and 'bad belle' will result in bad, dull, suspicious and domineering leadership that drives people with good intentions away from you. To lead others, you must first lead yourself well in your attitudes. You must acquire positive attitudes and jettison negative ones.

Healthy Leaders, Healthy Churches

e. Family

A godly and genuine leader must have a good home. Without a good home and family, you have no testimony in ministry. You must lead your home well if you are going to have the credibility to lead the church of God. True leadership in the church must start from your home. If it doesn't work well at home, it's useless exporting it abroad. Fight for your marriage. Be a good spouse to your partner. Raise up your children in the fear of the Lord and spend time to nurture your family in the Lord. Start at home and then the church can be properly led.

f. Relationships

Healthy leadership consists of ability to get along with others. Leadership doesn't have to be lonely, provided you know how to relate with others. Your relational abilities will also affect your leadership. If your relational skills are weak, your leadership will always suffer. Your ability to make friends and keep them over a long time is a pointer to your relational ability.

You must surely lead yourself very well in these mentioned areas, if you hope to lead powerfully. This principle means that your personal and inner growth will always show outwardly in your professional and ministerial growth. Growth of any kind begins with the leader. If you grow up, then

> *Your relational abilities will also affect your leadership. If your relational skills are weak, your leadership will always suffer.*

the work of God will grow in your hand. Our best preaching or ministry comes from the life that we are living, not the words we are speaking.

How to lead yourself well

When leaders fail to lead themselves, they shoot themselves in the foot. It is almost impossible to lead others well if you don't start with yourself. This is a lesson I've learnt very well and which have really helped me in the ministry. I'm constantly facing the challenge of leading myself and be a good model of those things that we teach to others in our ministry. To help you face the challenge of leading yourself first, you'll have to align with these factors:

1. Fellowship

To lead yourself well, you can't but be in constant fellowship with God and His Spirit. You must daily build time of fellowship with God through prayers, reading and studying the scriptures and worshipping in His sanctuary. True fellowship with God is crucial to personal leadership. It is your source of strength, grace, power and enablement. It will energize you and strengthen your inner man.

"That which we have seen and heard declare we unto you, that ye also may have fellowship with us: and truly our fellowship with the father, and with his son Jesus Christ" (I John 1:3).

Healthy leaders don't allow activities, busyness,

tiredness and weariness to hinder their time of fellowship with the Lord. They set aside time to commune and fellowship with the Lord and strive to maintain that time daily. The spiritual health of leaders depends on their time of fellowship with the Lord. The absence of it will lead to carnality, secular and unspiritual leadership that will lead the church nowhere.

2. Followership

You can't lead well, if you have not followed and continue to follow well. Leading yourself demands that you must have a leader. You must have someone as father, mentor, model and who you are accountable to. You need someone to speak to your life and who you can be reported to. You are not doing a good job of leading yourself well, when you are all-in-all and nobody can call you by your first name and speak to your life.

Abraham had Melchizedek, Moses had father Jethro and David had Prophet Samuel, Nathan and Gad. These Bible leaders allow these men to speak into their lives and they are accountable to them. You can't go far in true leadership without being accountable to a godly mentor. It is easier to fall away into error when you operate as an 'almighty minister'. It is easier to become an abusive leader when you cannot be reported to anybody and you have no fear for anyone. Leading yourself well entails being a good follower of the Lord and other godly leaders.

3. Focus and self development

For a long time, I've known the role of personal growth in the effort to lead oneself and I wrote a book on it, **"Personal Growth Today"**. To lead yourself, you'll have to embark on the journey of personal development. You must focus on your strengths and your weaknesses as well. You must never take yourself for granted. Rather, you must seek to improve and become better in your spiritual, emotional, social, mental and communication abilities. You must work on yourself in these areas, because if you don't, nobody else will. Your personal growth will be the growth of your work. Your personal growth will help you to become a better leader. Your improvement will help you to overcome your weak areas until they can no longer be your albatross.

> *Your personal growth will be the growth of your work. Your personal growth will help you to become a better leader.*

4. Allow the dealings of God

It takes time to become a healthy leader. It takes a long process and deep dealings of God to become the leader that is after the heart of God. God doesn't produce His leaders in microwave oven, but in a slow-cooker. He allows His leaders to pass through trials, tests and troubles that will sharpen and shape them for His glorious usage.

But too many leaders fail to lead themselves in this area due to their poor response to the dealings of God in their lives. They complain, murmur, rebel and denounce the formative hands of God through trials and seek for short-cuts. The fire of God that was meant to refine and purify them for His usage was denounced and the work of God had to stop. Such leaders eventually lead people to destruction, because something was terribly wrong with their preparation by God.

To really lead yourself well, you must allow God to deal with you in which ever way He chooses so that He can remove all the dirt and dross from your life. It is such dealings that will turn you into a true vessel of honour, fit for the Master's use. The dealings of God are not once and for all, rather, it is life long, provided you are tender, surrendered and pliable in His hand. The more He works in you, the more He can work through you. Therefore, be patient with God in your life and be patient with yourself.

5. Self discipline

While self-indulgence is the law of death, self-discipline is the law of life. You can only lead yourself if you practise self-discipline. To deny yourself of self-gratification and control your emotions is the great mark of a disciplined person. You'll have to say no to the wrong feelings, appetite and desires that well up within your flesh. You'll have to put a bridle to your mouth and pinch yourself when you are tempted to lust with your eyes.

"He that hath no rule over his own spirit is like a city that is broken down, and without walls." (Proverbs 25:28).

To lead yourself, you must master your eyes, mouth, tongue, emotions and spirit. You must be in control of yourself in every situation. Though this is very hard and difficult to achieve, yet that is what you must do as a leader, if you are going to lead yourself well. An undisciplined leader is not worth a dime in the market!

Vitamin 'L'S of Leadership

If you don't examine yourself, people will not respect you as a leader. In your effort to truly lead yourself, you'll have to examine yourself whether you possess these vitamins. Vitamins are daily doses that we need to remain in top physical health. Without them, we become infirm and sickly. It's the same in our spiritual leadership. You'll always need these vitamin 'L's, if you are going to be a spiritually healthy leader. By taking care of yourself everyday with these vitamins, you'll be able to lead yourself very well.

1. Life

Your life is your leadership. There is no leadership outside the life you are living. You can never live wrong and hope to lead right. It is absolutely impossible. The power behind your leadership is the life you are living. Remember, leadership has more to do with your person than with your position. You must always lead yourself before you can lead others. Therefore, lead from the power of your life. Live right, godly and purposefully and see your leadership affecting others positively.

2. Limit

It is not whether you have limits; it is what you are going to do with them. Healthy leaders don't allow their limits to serve as limitations over their lives and ministries. They work at removing them. Limits can be internal or external. Internal limits are fear, inferiority complex, anger, jealousy and a particular sin. And external limits are financial crisis, low education, opposition and criticism from friends and foes. It is your duty to work over these limits in your life.

A good leader must continually work at removing every limit that tends to limit him and his leadership. You must recognize your lid and work at removing them before they become your limitation.

3. Look

It is possible to look without seeing. The eyes that look are common, but the eyes that see are rare. Healthy leaders look to see. They see before, see more, see higher and see deeper than others. Their eyes are as strong as that of the eagle bird. They don't only look but they also see clearly, concisely and captivatingly. Healthy leaders are seers and they communicate what they see to others in simple and relevant way.

4. Love

Healthy leaders are motivated by genuine love, care, burden and desire to bring about change. They are not motivated by title, position, fame, power and wealth. Love must always be the motivating factor in leadership. Until you lead out of true love, you are not really a leader. Love for the glory of God, for humanity and love to contribute positively to kingdom advancement must be uppermost in the heart of healthy leaders. It is only when you are motivated by genuine love to serve and help others that you are really leading.

5. Listen

Listening is an art that must be learned by great leaders. Good leaders are listeners. They have ears to hear and listen to God first and then others. Healthy leaders develop their ability to listen well to those very close to them. They are not self-willed and arrogant. They are not too preoccupied with their own ideas that they don't listen to others. Rather, they listen to better ideas, counsel and suggestions from associates and team members. Listening to associates and making adjustments where necessary always bring respect and commitment from them.

People also listen to good leaders. They listen because of integrity, performance, experience, care and sincerity by the leader. If you want to be the leader that others will listen to, then lead yourself to listen clearly to God first and listen attentively to your associates too.

6. Learn

Healthy leaders must be learners. The more you learn the better you become. If you stop learning, you start to lean. You cannot provide true and dynamic leadership without a learning spirit. Leaders that are too proud to learn and continue learning will soon expire in ministry. Leaders grow stale and fade away in ministry simply because they lose their learning spirit.

There is no position, title, achievement and attainment in life that should keep you from learning from both the young and old, high and low. It is impossible to be a candle within and hope to shine like a halogen light outside. What you know is what will make you known, and what takes you there will never keep you there.

7. Light

Every leader must shine as true light. Your light must shine brightly for others to see. Healthy leaders bring light and illumination to others. They show good examples and model. Their leadership dispel darkness in the life and family of others. True leaders are lights and there is no darkness in them at all.

However, healthy leaders are not shallow, fickle, light and content-free leaders. They have spiritual depth and spirituality. A light leader will be a yo-yo leader who looks deep far away, but is so shallow when you get close. Such leaders lose the respect and deep admiration of people.

8. Lifter

The purpose of leadership is to lift others up. Leaders, like mountain climbers, derive joy in helping others get to the top. A healthy leader therefore must be a lifter, not a limiter of people. He must use his ministry and leadership to raise people to become good, highly successful and worthy men and women. A great leader is not someone only at the top, he does everything to lift others to the top also.

The leader as a lifter spends time, talent and treasures to equip, empower and enable others to

Healthy Leaders, Healthy Churches

discover and fulfill their potentials. He is the cheer leader of the gifts and graces of others and he is in the front clapping with genuine joy when the gifts of others are being celebrated. Healthy leaders give their platform to others so that they too will be lifted up.

9. Ladder

In the same vein, a healthy leader is a ladder. He provides the way, connection and passage for others to climb up. He provides a good shoulder for others to climb on for greater view. He takes joy in being a developer of talent and graces of others. He provides the training, resources, opportunities and chance for people to climb up. He is free from jealousy and envy. He is like John the Baptist, who declares concerning Jesus, "*He must increase, but I must decrease*" (John 3:30). A healthy leader sees his primary duty as that of a ladder, he rests on God and others can rest on him to climb up.

10. Labour

Healthy leadership is hard work. A lazy and indolent person cannot provide healthy and great leadership. A great leader labours hard and toils long to provide result and production. A genuine leader works harder and smarter than others. Yes, he delegates but he also rolls up his sleeves and labour hard. He knows that hard work is still needed to succeed as a leader. He labours in secret prayers and the word. He labours to provide training resources to leaders and bring others up in the Lord. Spiritually lazy leaders cannot do a great work for the Lord.

11. Levels

There are levels for everything. There are levels of grace, power, blessing, anointing and favour. There is also a level in leadership and ministry impact. Every genuine and healthy leader seeks to take the work to another level. He works and prays for higher dimension of impact, effect, transformation and effectiveness of the church and ministry.

Healthy leaders are not satisfied with the status-quo. They seek to bring higher dimension of impact to the work. They thank God for the present level, but their heart and desire is for higher level of effectiveness.

12. Landmark

Leaders must seek to leave veritable landmarks and legacy for God and society. Leaders cannot lead forever. Leadership is an opportunity to make impact and leave indelible mark in the lives of people and society. The greatest landmark is to bring positive transformation to the lives, family, finances and spiritual lives of those you come in contact with. It is to spend your resources to equip many, develop some and mentor few. Knowing that when you raise men, then you will not be erased from the earth.

Fine structures, buildings and cathedrals will collapse. Wealth will grow wings and fly away, but raising men and successors that will be able to raise others is an unforgettable legacy of any leadership.

13. Landmines

Every leader must beware of leadership landmines. They have blown away many and they are still around to blow away those who are careless and carefree in their leadership. Landmines are small bombs that are placed carefully on the ground. They are not designed to kill, but to incapacitate those who are careless.

Generally speaking, females, fund and fame or women, wealth and wine are recognized as the landmine of leadership. However, there are other little ones that ruin leaders quickly too, such as covetousness, lying, false doctrine and idolatory. Run from them or else, they will blow you away in no time. Healthy leaders watch themselves carefully so as to avoid the landmines of leadership.

A Chinese proverb says, *'the greatest watchman in the world is the man that watches himself'*. And *'the careful foot can walk anywhere'*

You will always do a good job of leading yourself very well, when you daily take doses of these vitamins. It is your responsibility to lead yourself first, before you can have the moral and spiritual strength to lead others. It is your duty to **'work out your own salvation with fear and trembling'** (Phil. 2:12). Also, you must **"look to yourselves, that we lose not those things which we have wrought, but that we receive a full reward."** (II John 8)

Healthy Leaders, Healthy Churches

TAKE HOME

Ponder on these questions to improve yourself.

1. Do you now believe that your greatest challenge as a leader is to lead your very self well?

2. How have you been leading yourself in those salient areas a leader should lead himself first?

3. As a leader, do you have someone leading you? If not, get a godly leader and mentor today.

4. How do you react to God's dealing in your life as a leader?

5. How often do you take the Vitamin 'L's of leadership?

NOTE

These vitamins are daily doses a leader must take to be healthy.

Capacity of Leaders, Capacity of Churches

"When leaders stop improving, churches start to decrease."

A certain pastor was concerned with the stagnant state of his church and he decided to seek the face of God in prayer in a secluded mountain. After bombarding heaven with intensive prayers for growth in his church for days, he heard the Lord telling him; *"your church cannot grow because you are not growing. Go back home and grow first, then your church will start to grow."* He had to come back home to improve his capacity to handle the growth he is anticipating in his church.

The issue of leadership capacity is very vital to the growth, progress, prevailing and productive nature of churches. Manufacturers don't joke with this factor in their vehicles, planes, carriages and products. Failure to abide by capacity utilization has led to disasters and problems of great proportions.

A commercial Jetliner crashed on Christmas Day in 2003 in Benin Republic. 200 bodies of Lebanese businessmen who were going to Bethlehem on that day were picked up from the Atlantic Ocean where the plane crashed immediately after take off. Investigation later showed that the plane was overloaded with human and material cargo, well beyond the capacity of the aircraft. The more reason for the crash and subsequent loss of precious lives.

In the same vein, churches and ministries cannot fly beyond the capacity and ability of their leaders. Any attempt to lead the church beyond the capability of the leaders will result in crash-landing and consequences of great proportions.

Human and divine partnership

Church growth and health is not like a ripe paw-paw that falls down form heaven without effort on our part. Rather, it's both a human and divine partnership. As the Apostle Paul says in I Corinthians 3:6, "*I have planted, Apollos watered; but God gave the increase.*" Paul and Apollos must plant and water before God will bring the much needed increase. True growth, revival and fruitfulness in the church comes from God, but human vessels must make the conditions right first before God will send the growth.

In reality, your capacity is your growth. The capacity of the church will be determined by the capacity of the leaders. If your leadership ability, capacity and capability can only handle 50 people, you cannot see 100 people under your leadership. Your degree of fruitfulness will largely be determined by your capacity. The inability of a church to move further is the inability of the leadership.

Capacity building for leaders

The largest Airplane in history is called A380. It can carry 800 passengers at a go and will land at a five kilometer run way. The point of touch down must be 10 times ticker than the normal aircraft. In the last four years, major airports around the world have continued to build and increase their airport capacity to handle the A380 airplane. But it cannot come to Nigeria yet, because we don't have the capacity to handle it. Our runway is only 3 kilometer long and arrival hall cannot handle such large volume of passengers from a single aircraft!

> *In reality, your capacity is your growth. The capacity of the church will be determined by the capacity of the leaders.*

Leaders will be unable to see greater blessings of God upon their lives and ministries when they don't embark on capacity building in their leadership. Even if you are not yet in leadership position, you can improve your capacity. If you start preparing when you are already a leader, you are too late.

Capacity is defined as ability to do, contain and hold. It is the skill and competent ability to do things well. It is

Healthy Leaders, Healthy Churches

the enablement to be effective and result oriented. Capacity, ability and capability can be divine, learned and developed. It is not static. It can be improved, honed and polished for maximum effectiveness.

"But other fell on a good ground, and brought forth fruit, some an hundredfold, some sixty fold, some thirty fold." (Matt. 13:8)

In this scripture, the sower sowed the good seed on the ground. The problem is not with the sower, nor with the seed. The ground was good but the seed brought forth in 100, 60, and 30 folds. Why? The capacity of the ground was different, that is why it produced at different levels. To produce at thirty, sixty or hundred fold is largely determined by your capability.

Father Jethro also advised Moses to choose leaders of identical qualities but should give them responsibilities according to their capacities. While some can handle tens, others can handle fifties and hundreds, while some outstanding ones can be leaders of thousands. While their calling, anointing and positions are the same, their individual capacities made the huge difference in their leadership. (Exodus 18:19-21). To move from being a leader of ten to fifty, hundred and thousands is dependent on your increased capacities. Remember, God will not give you more than you can handle.

> *Capacity, ability and capability can be divine, learned and developed.*

Why leaders capacity must improve

Healthy leaders always work to improve their spiritual, leadership, mental, relational, emotional and communication capacities, knowing fully well that their effectiveness depends on it. Without capacity improvement, your ministry will shrink and stagnate. Let me mention some points to underscore the absolute necessity of capacity improvement for leaders.

- Your church or ministry will always be a replica of your leadership
- You can never shine more than the light you have.
- God's blessing over you is limited by your capacity to receive. (I Kings 4:1-7)
- You cannot lead more than you have gone yourself.
- You cannot give what you don't have.
- The work will never go to the next level when you remain at the same level.
- The more you improve; the better will be your work.
- Where better is possible, good is not good enough.
- Where best is possible, better is not better enough.
- Where excellence is possible, best is not best enough.
- You will never be productive beyond your capacity

So many leaders' ability and capabilities remain the same year after year as a result of the following:

1. Believe In providence

When leaders believe that their churches will grow whenever God wants it, they will never see the need to work on themselves. When a leader's mindset is waiting upon God for one big breakthrough, then he will not improve himself to bring it about. Why? Because it is the work of God and he will do it at His own time.

2. Prejudice against learning and growing:

Many leaders cannot improve because they are prejudiced against learning and castigate books. They believe that the Bible is the only book they should read.

3 Relying on position and power:

Too many leaders assume that once they have the position and power, then they are okay. They lead from the power of their position and that will only be for a while. Leaders that fail to improve their capacity will lead the church down and will eventually lose their position.

4 Inability to change and grow:

Leaders cannot improve their capacity because they fail to change and grow. They fight and resist growth, both in their personal and corporate lives. They hold on to tradition and heritage, rather than being forward looking. Because leaders capacity remain the same, churches too remain stagnant, struggling and eventually nose dive.

Leaders cannot lead further than they have gone themselves. Despite fasting, prayers and knowledge acquisition, if they don't lead to increased capabilities, churches will continue to flounder and experience downward spiral.

How to increase your capacity

Here are time – tested and proven ways to improve your capacity, thereby increasing the capability of your church and ministry:

1   Pursue growth everyday

It is not I am going to grow, but it is the growth you are experiencing everyday. Growth must be a daily thing. You must grow better today than you were yesterday. The more you grow the better you become and the more you are able to do for God. Every leader that desires increased capacity must engage in the journey of deliberate, consistent and constant personal growth. If you do not grow within, you cannot grow without.

The most difficult thing to do in life is to try to change the outside result without first changing the inner ability. It is the inner ability that determines the external capacity. Your level of private preparation will always determine the level of your public performance.

2   Go for training, enroll for courses

Continuous learning is always the key to increase your mind. The size of your mind is the size of your capacity. When you stop increasing your mind, your capacity will definitely stop. Your life cannot achieve what your mind cannot conceive.

No man will mind a man without a working mind. Therefore learn by reading, enrolling for relevant courses, re-training in your field and generally improving your mental capacity. Learn by listening and asking questions. Have a teachable spirit and be humble enough to learn from all. When the appetite for learning is no longer there, the tendency for decrease is 100% sure.

3. Deliberate discipline

Indiscipline has been noted as the greatest killer of working capacity. When you cannot discipline your vessel, you will lose your virtue. When you cannot discipline your eyes, you will lose your sight. When you cannot discipline your appetite you will lose your heritage.

Life of discipline is not popular but it is the key to real popularity.

Discipline is the key to the multiplication of every leader's capacity. Life of discipline is not easy but it is compulsory for success. Life of discipline is not popular but it is the key to real popularity. Life of discipline is very narrow but it leads to the best mansion in heaven. Life of discipline is unattractive but it is the channel to real attraction.

4. Move with those who can challenge you

Psychologists have discovered that a person on grade three brain level can move to grade seven brain level within a period of one year, if he begins to move with people in grade seven level. The same goes for every church leader who wants to build up his working capacity. Just look for other leaders who are operating at a better level than you and start relating with them. Learn from them and within a short time, your working capacity will be built up. Association determines destination. Show me your friends and I will tell you your strength.

5. Constant communion with The Holy Spirit

There is a great revelation of how every church leader can build himself up through fellowship with the Holy Spirit in Jude 1:20 ***"But you, building up yourself on your most holy faith, praying in the Holy Ghost."***

Constant and regular fellowship with the Holy Spirit is a master key to building up your spiritual capacity as a leader. When you take the Holy Spirit for granted, you will definitely be grounded. Your level of activity must march the level of your spirituality for maximum productivity.

6. Dynamic prayer life

All great leaders for God have learnt to engage in active, revelational, inspiring and dynamic prayer life. Elijah was a man subject to like passion like us but there is one thing that increased his capacity better than many of us. He knew how to pray fervent and effective prayers. Prayer has a way of increasing your spiritual capacity. Remember, it is the capacity of church leaders that determine the growth capacity of any church.

We must be persistent in prayer for God to be consistent in action. The declining of your working capacity is the supernatural evidence of your neglect of prayer. When you neglect prayer, growth and increase will neglect you. You can acquire the capacity you desire if you perspire in prayer and you do not retire.

7. Face challenges and handle them

Nothing have the ability to increase your capacity much more than problem handling. You must grow to a level whereby you are no longer afraid of problems. You must become proactive, not reactionary to problems and the problematic person. You must develop the capacity to handle problems in a matured, balanced, impartial and edifying way. You must stop being moody, downcast, crest fallen and thrown-off balance by problems. Your problem handling skills is a clear pointer to your level of ability.

On a final note, it is absolutely impossible to move a church forward without capacity improvement on the part of church leaders and workers. Leadership ability increase is always the key to any organizational increase.

If your church will move from 200, 500, 1000 membership to 5,000 members, then you must get ready to improve your own leadership capacity as well as that of your associates and workers. You must change their perspective, enlarge their vision, review their motives, strengthen their attitudes, increase their experiences, empower their hearts and equip their hands to work. It is then and only then the church will move to the next level. The capacity of leaders is always the capacity of churches.

TAKE HOME

Ponder on these questions to improve your leadership.

1. What is the level of your capacity and capability presently?

2. How do you intend to build on and improve your capacity?

NOTE

If you don't improve on your capacity and capability now, when are you going to do it?

Healthy Leaders, Healthy Churches

Chapter Two

The Rise And Fall of Churches

Relationship: The heart of Leadership

"If your relational skills are weak, your leadership will always suffer"

A particular Bishop was very harsh and hostile to his drummer boy in the church. He made life very difficult for him and used every opportunity to castigate and maltreat the boy. People that knew were surprised that there was no love between them. When the boy could no longer bear it, he decided to leave.

Years later, the Lord called him and he grew to become a wonderful church leader. Then he met face to face with his old Bishop at a meeting where they were both guest speakers. The old Bishop could not look up at his face, nor respond warmly to his greetings. He remembered all he had done to the boy. He later confessed that he never imagine that the boy would one day grow to become an important church leader. Well, the lesson? Don't ever look down on anybody. The seed of today is the oak tree of tomorrow!

> *Don't ever look down on anybody. The seed of today is the oak tree of tomorrow!*

The heart is the center of our being. It pumps gallons of blood to every part of your being in minutes. If your hand, feet or legs are affected somehow, you can still live well. But when your heart is affected, then you are gone. Indeed and in truth, the ability to relate with various kinds of people is at the very heart of leadership.

Rockfeller said that *"he is more willing to pay more for this quality than for any other ability under the sun"*. President Roosevelt said, *"It was the most important ingredient in the formula of success."* That quality is your ability to relate with people. More than almost anything in life and ministry, relationships can make or break us.

In the scripture (I Samuel 25:1-42), there is the story of Abigail and Nabal her husband. Abigail was able to save her family from destruction because she knew how to demonstrate her relational skills with David. She showed wit, humility, generosity, selfless attitude, courage and personal responsibility. Contra wise, her husband, Nabal was a prototype of pastors and church leaders of today.

We become so consumed with our work and personal life that we neglect the only eternal resource on earth: people. We use, dump, neglect, distrust, disrespect, devalue and careless about people. the more reason our leadership is suffering and will continue to suffer until we learn how to truly relate with people.

In my interaction with and observation of leaders over the last 14 years, I have come to discover that the average church leader have very poor relational skills. Most pastors are not taught this subject in Bible Schools and many leaders come into ministry with the sole idea of ruling, using and dominating people. Relationship and relational skills are always at the lowest rung of the ladder in pastoral priorities. But we must realize that relationship and relational skills are paramount to the kingdom of God.

I am fully convinced that every church leader must develop, hone and continually sharpen their relational skills. Simply put, relationship is the ability to get along with various kinds of people and go along with them. If you can't get along with them, they won't go along with you. Church is all about people, not properties and structures. Leaders are in the people business. Leaders will always need people and leadership requires people oriented skills.

Relational skill of leaders

Emmanuel is the name of the Lord – God with us. He relates with us, if not, we would all rot in hell. Jesus was a Master relationship maker. He related with various kinds of people. He related with the poor, wealthy, children, women, unworthy sinners, doctors of the law and everyone He came across. He showed to us that leaders can accomplish much more with their relational skills than with force, coercion and dictatorial tendencies.

Faith revolves around relationships; vertical with God and horizontal with people. Every healthy leader must develop and maintain a vibrant vertical relationship with God on a daily basis. Nothing must be allowed to break your relationship with God. He must be first and all in your life. He must be your strength, power, source and spring. Your relationship with God is the mainstay of your life as a leader.

Your relationship with people must be horizontal too. The more you relate with God, the better must be your relationship with people. If your relational skills are weak, your leadership will always suffer. Your ability to get along with people will determine your success or failure as a leader. Getting people to like you is merely the other side of liking them.

> *Your ability to get along with people will determine your success or failure as a leader.*

Relationship are formed, not forced or forged. 'You cannot shake hands with a clenched fist'. You'll have to show yourself friendly before you can attract friends. 'If you love your opinion more than your brethren, you will defend your opinion but destroy your brethren.' 'If you want to go fast, go alone. But if you want to go far, go together.'

People are always the greatest asset of leadership. The leadership that doesn't place great value on people will not last. Leaders must realize and understand this simple relationship mathematics that R+R-R=R+R. Meaning; Rules plus Regulations minus Relationship equals to Resentment and Rebellion.

When you love to make rules and regulations without relating with people, then you'll have lots of resentment and rebellion from your people. That is the negative side of it.

Here is the positive side: R+R+R=R+R. Meaning; Rules plus Regulations plus Relationship equals to Respect and Result. While you are giving out the rules and regulations of the ministry, take time to relate with people too. Then they will respect you and give you the result you so much desire.

Relationship must always be for the mutual benefit of both the leader and the people. It must uplift, encourage, motivate, inspire, enable and empower both parties.

To build great relational skills with people, every church leader must possess these three attributes:

1. Have a leader's head – Understand people:

Here are ten things you must understand about people:

a. People are insecure – give them confidence

b. People like to feel special – sincerely compliment them

c. People are basically selfish – speak to their needs

first

d. People look for better tomorrow — show them hope

e. People want to be understood — listen to them

f. People lack direction — navigate for them

g. People get emotionally low — encourage them

h. People want to be successful — help them win

i. People desire meaningful relationship — provide community

j. People seek models to follow — be an example for them.

2. Have a leader's heart – Love people:

Show people that you care and love them. Demonstrate in no uncertain terms that your motive of leading is not money but genuine love for the people. It is true that you can't love and antagonize people at the same time.

If you secretly detest and hate the people, despite your public show of love, it will surface in your actions and people will smell your motives miles away. When you don't love people genuinely, you will attract cunning and crafty people. You play them, they play you. Love for God and His people must ooze out of you before you can build good and great relationship with people.

3. Have a leader's hand – Help people:

Building good relationship with your people demands that you must lend a helping hand to them always. You must provide opportunities and chance for them to rise to the top. You must equip and assist them to fulfill their potentials. You must give them challenge and chance to perform. Your helping hand must never be weary to under gird and support them.

If you can possess the leaders head, heart and hand, then you can be a leader with good relational skills and your work can move to the next level. Remember, without vision, the people perish. Also, without people, the vision equally perishes. (Proverbs 29:18)

Why leaders don't relate well

"Now we exhort you, brethren, warn them that are unruly, comfort the feebleminded, support the weak, be patient toward all men" (I Thess 5:14)

The scripture commands leaders to relate with various kinds of men in the church. But the reality is that most church leaders are very poor in their relationships with people, their members, staff and the communities where their churches are located. They tend to talk and behave anyhow, thinking that they are doing the people favour by leading them. Well, such leaders have experienced lots of backdoor losses. Why is it that church leaders don't relate well with people? The following factors will show:

a. Wrong training and teaching emphasis:

Many myths and wrong teachings given to leaders in preparatory schools, seminaries and school of ministries have contributed greatly to lack of relational skill of leaders. One of them says: '*if you are too close to people, they will no longer respect you.*' Another one says '*People are expendables, just use them as ladder for your rising and dump them.*' These wrong myths have greatly hindered leaders from relating well with people.

b. Poor self image:

The wrong image you have of yourself restricts your ability to build healthy relationships. A negative self image will keep you from loving and accepting others. The most important relationship you will ever have is with yourself. You must be your own best friend. If you don't like yourself, how can you like and befriend others?

c. Wrong temperament:

Leaders that are easily angry and given to fits of temper will find relationship very challenging. Quick and volatile temper doesn't make for lasting relationships.

d. Past experiences:

Many leaders find relationship with their people very difficult simply because of past experiences with unfaithful, disloyal and deceptive associates. Their past experiences have left them with too many wounds and scars that disallow them from relating with new people.

Past injuries and hurts leave them with unforgiving spirit, bitter hearts and suspicion of people's intentions

.e. Superiority complex:

Some leaders are unable to relate with their associates because they are afflicted with superiority complex disease. They have a large ego and they are proud of their place, race, face, grace, pace and they make lots of pretense.

These factors have blunted the relational skill of leaders. Leaders who do not relate well will find it hard to move ahead in the ministry.

Four levels of Relationships

1. Surface level

No strong commitment – just saying hello to each other. You look at each other from a distance and only exchange glances. Though with no reward, yet it is the foundation of all other levels.

2. Structured level

This is triggered off by routine encounters. They may be tied to a specific place or time. Common interest or activities might cause it. They are also called casual relationships. Frequent encounters will lead to casual greetings and talking together in an informal way. Some will remain at this level, but majority always move to the next level.

3. Secure level

This is sharing together as a result of reaching a level of comfort with each other. You develop trust and desire to share time together. Friendship is developed and tested at this level. You hold each other to trust and sincere friendship.

4. Solid relationship

This is the highest and deepest form of all relationships. It occurs when people share complete trust and confidentiality in one another. They lead to desire to serve and give to one another and the forging of long term relationships.

The fact of the matter today is that people are lonely in the ministry because they spend their times building walls instead of building bridges. When leaders build walls, they enclose and cut themselves off from others. But when they build bridges, they reach out and connect with others.

> *When leaders build walls, they enclose and cut themselves off from others. But when they build bridges, they reach out and connect with others.*

Sadly, many leaders are known relationship breakers. I've had cause to tell one of such pastors to his face. He breaks relationships at will. Even those relationships that God have used to uplift his life and ministry. Such pastors always go down in life and ministry, because one relationship with the right person can make or break you. Even though you have to break a secure or solid relationship, close that door very gently, since you might have to go through it again!

Learn to relate with those who are under you, those who are your colleagues and those who are above you.

Ten kinds of men you must lead

Leaders must know how to lead various kinds of men and women in the church. Your ability to handle these different kinds of men will determine your success. Different men and women will want to pull the church in different directions. Every person has ideas on how the church should be led. But it is your responsibility as a leader to study and know each kind of men and lead them to embrace your leadership of the vision God had given to the church. Let's see them:-

Kinds of men	Characteristics	Strategy
1. The power-brokers	Ride over people	Stand up to them when necessary
2. The Religious bigots	Pretenders and hypocrite	Confront and demand repentance
3. The unrealistic men	Perfectionist, criticizes every thing	Bring them to reality
4. The Volcano	Explosive, unpredictable	Remove from crowd, be direct.
5. The Thumb-sucker	Self pity and petty	Do not reward but expose them to challenges.
6. The wet-blanket	Always down and moody.	Be honest, don't let them lead.

Healthy Leaders, Healthy Churches

7. The garbage collector	Attracts the worst, dumpsite.	Challenge their claims, face honesty.
8. The chameleon	Deceptive and tempetous	Protect yourself and show carefulness.
9. The User	Demands for attention.	Set boundaries, demand accountability
10. The Sunshine	Always up and helpful.	Do not overuse and over depend.

Leaders must know how to relate with these kinds of people in the church and lead them aright; else, they will turn the church into something else. You'll need lots of courage, faith, confidence and relational skills to do that. You must be tough and tender in your relational skills to achieve that.

Human Relational Skills

1. Smile to people -   Your dressing is not ccomplete until you put on a smile.

2. Speak to people -   The tone and tenor of your voice matters.

3. Call people by name -   It shows you are thoughtful

4. Be friendly and helpful - It will open doors for you.

5. Be cordial - Respect begat respect.

6. Have genuine interest in people - People can smell your intentions miles away.

7. Be generous with praise - Sarcastic people don't draw good people.

8. Be considerate of the feeling of others - It makes you a pleasant fellow.

9. Be thoughtful of the opinion of others - It shows you are not full of yourself.

10. Be alert to give service - It is your doorway to success.

TAKE HOME

Ponder on these questions to improve yourself.

1. How good are you at relating with people?

2. How have you been handling your relationship with the different kinds of people that come under your leadership?

Chapter Two

The Rise And Fall of Churches

Competent Pastoral Leaders Today

"Incompetent leaders have done much more damage to the church"

In a certain denominational church, a Pastor was recently transferred to a local branch. On his resumption day, he was surprised to see the doors of the church locked and the members outside with placards protesting that they didn't want him. Obviously, they had heard his negative impact in his last church, the more reason they rejected him, though in an unorthodox way. But the truth of this real life story is that pastors are being rejected today.

Competence has become a serious issue in pastoral ministry today. Lots and lots of pastoral leaders are being rejected and people are leaving churches because they can no longer put up with incompetent pastors.

Crisis of incompetent pastoral leaders

In a rough estimate, over 80% of pastoral leaders are incompetent one way or the other, the more reason for large percentage of small, sick, struggling and stagnant churches all around us today. Too many denominational and independent churches have aggravated the situation by throwing competency to the dogs when pastors are being placed over churches.

Incompetent pastors are the reason for large number of squalid churches today. Incompetent pastors are unmarketable, irrelevant, outdated, archaic, non-current and outmoded pastoral leaders who lead churches in ways that lead to stagnation and downward spiral. The greatest barrier to church health and wholesomeness is incompetent pastors.

The number one illness and terminal disease of churches, is ungodly, non-growing, low capacity, weak, sick, spiritually poor and carnal pastoral leaders. An incompetent Pastor is the first wrong signal of a bleak future for any church. The large majority of the church have become a laughing stock in the eyes of the world today due to the activities of wrong, sinful, half-baked, and

> *The number one illness and terminal disease of churches, is ungodly, non-growing, low capacity, weak, sick, spiritually poor and carnal pastoral leaders.*

Healthy Leaders, Healthy Churches

uncooked pastors. The church has been worse for it when pastors are incompetent.

Today, we have pastors who are preaching; *'if God will mark iniquity, who shall escape' 'in my church I don't make people uncomfortable by talking about sin.'* Such pastoral leaders gather religious people and they are a disgrace to the true church. It's time each of us starts working on our competency level in pastoral ministry like never before. Because, if the church is going to be healthy, dynamic and on fire for God, then pastoral leaders must update and upgrade their competency level.

Competent pastoral leader

Wanted urgently – dynamic, effective, godly and competent pastoral leaders that will lead the church to the next level of impact. The Lord promised to provide such pastors for His church. ***"And I will give you pastors according to mine heart, which shall feed you with knowledge and understanding."*** (Jeremiah 3:15)

A competent Pastor is a productive, well-equipped and marketable leader that practically led the church forward. To be competent is to have enough skill or knowledge to do a task well or to the necessary standard. It is not acquired in a day but over a period of time. Competence is both a spiritual quality and learned skill. Spiritual, mental, social and psychological competence must be in the life and leadership of the pastor of today. A truly competent pastor is God's man in God's church in God's time with growing skills to lead the church to higher ground of God's promises.

Pastoral leaders must be highly competent today because the work of the ministry is much more complex than ever before. Highly complex, intelligent and educated people are coming to the church much more than ever before. Sinners are becoming more sophisticated by the day. Technology and advancement is taking place rapidly in the world. In the midst of all these, it will take real competent skills from pastors to build up healthy, growing and glorious churches that will become rapturable today.

Pastoral leaders must be highly competent today because the work of the ministry is much more complex than ever before.

The future of the work will always depend on the competency that the leader is displaying. Competent Pastors will always translate to contagious churches. It is now glaring that churches cannot move forward when pastors are largely incompetent and ineffective. Healthy churches are always the outcome of healthy and competent pastoral leaders.

Multiple competency in pastoral leaders

Healthy churches call for highly competent pastoral leaders. Any kind of pastor will not do. Gone are the days when pastoral leaders are competent in one area only and they are leading churches. Not any more!

Pastoral leaders must show and display competence in several areas.

Every pastoral leader that wants to gauge his competence must measure himself against the qualities I'm going to enumerate below. You must be growing and maturing in these foundational areas, both in your life and ministry before you can say you are becoming a competent pastoral leader.

Relationship is the best way of measuring them. You must be growing in your relationship in these areas. You must daily grow into them and in them. Every local church must have pastoral leaders who are highly competent in these areas:

1. Growing in relationship with God

This is the first and foundational area to show competence. You must be growing in your relationship with God. You must know the Lord in a personal and intimate way. You must be a true son before you become a minister.

Your calling as a son, *"Come unto me all ye that labor and are heavy laden and I will give you rest"* (Matt 11:28) is much more important than your calling as a minister. You must know Him before you can show Him to others. You must love God above everything else.

"Jesus said unto him, thou shalt love the Lord thy God with all thy heart, and with all thy soul, and with all thy mind. This is the first and great commandment." (Matt.22:37-38)

Part of your competency in this area is that you are filled with the Spirit and growing in fellowship with Him. You are able to discern the will of God and His voice in every situation. You earnestly pursue His glory in what you do and expand His kingdom. Your relationship with God must be growing daily and dynamic, because it is your spirituality that will affect that work.

When your relationship with the Lord is cold, lukewarm and stagnant, it will surely lead to low spiritual thermometer of the church. Pastoral leaders that have lost their relationship with God will always lead the church into carnality and worldliness.

> *Pastoral leaders that have lost their relationship with God will always lead the church into carnality and worldliness.*

When your love has waxed cold and God is no longer number one in your heart and life, then the church will take a downward turn spiritually and physically. When you are out of touch with God, either as a result of too much activities or a sin, then the negative effect will be on the church. Churches always suffer whenever the pastoral leader is no longer fervent, lively and vibrant in his relationship with God.

2. Growing in relationship with himself

It is mandatory that you know yourself and have a very good image of yourself. Your self – identity is very crucial to your success in ministry. If you don't like and accept the way God has made you, how can you be of help to those you are leading? Free yourself from every inferiority or superiority complex. Accept the way God has wired you and be at peace. If you are not at peace with yourself, you can never be at peace with others. Master your emotions and have control over yourself.

Inculcate godly character and Christian values into your life. Work over your weak areas and capitalize on your strengths. Maintain and imbibe spiritual disciplines and be a good steward of your time, talent and treasures. Put your body in subjection and learn to lead yourself very well. If you are not competent in leading yourself, how can you be competent enough to lead others?

"But I keep under my body, and bring it into subjection; lest that by any means, when I have preached to others, I myself should be a cast away." (I Cor.9:27)

You must have personal success before ministry success. You must succeed in leading yourself first, before you can succeed in leading others. You must keep growing and working over yourself.

3. Growing in relationship with his family.

As a pastoral leader, you cannot afford to fail in your home and family. A doctor, lawyer, an engineer or government official might have physical success without a good home and family, but not a pastoral leader.

"One that ruleth well his own house, having his children in subjection with all gravity. For if a man know not how to rule his own house, how shall he take care of the church of God?" (I Tim 3:4-5)

You must honor and value the family institution. You must place priority on having a good home. Choose your partner prayerfully and carefully. Pray and seek the face of God intensively before you dabble into marriage. Once you have married, do everything to stay married.

Grow in love towards your partner and relate well with your children. Grow to become a godly partner, a great lover and responsible parent to your kids. Learn to confront every marital challenge with prayers, patience and perseverance in God. Do everything to make your marriage a model to others. Display competence in handling your home affairs and people will give you the permission to handle their own homes too.

4. Growing in relationship with his leaders

You must show competence in the way you relate with your leaders and mentors. A godly pastoral leader have leaders and mentors. You must be the son of somebody and be under the mentorship of a godly leader.

"For this cause have I sent unto you Timotheus, who is my beloved son, and faithful in the Lord, who shall bring you into remembrance of my ways which be in Christ, as I teach everywhere in every church." (I Cor.4:17).

You must love the leaders that God has given to you and be obedient, teachable and faithful to them. Honour, respect and value must be placed on the leaders that are above you in the Lord. You must stop being individualistic in your ministry, but become a team player.

It is mandatory that you submit to authority and become accountable to a godly mentor. Let people know who your father is. Whom you submit to and who you can be reported to. The centurion said to Jesus, **"For I am a man under authority…"** (Matt.8:9). Under whose authority are you?

5. Growing in relationship with his flock

Competent pastoral leaders must handle the flock of God carefully. It is His flock, not your flock. So, careful handling and competent leadership is highly required.

"Take heed therefore unto yourselves and to all the flock, over the which the Holy Ghost hath made you overseers, to feed the church of God, which he hath purchased with His own blood." (Acts 20:28)

Your relationship with the flock of God is very crucial. It must be a relationship that is borne out of a vision to build a healthy people and church for the Lord. It means you must grow to a pastor, servant, mentor, instructor, prophet, father, builder and leader to them. You must love, forgive and forbear with them as you lead them and having a growing relationship that will make them follow you to fulfill the vision of a healthy church.

Healthy Leaders, Healthy Churches

You must demonstrate competence as you try to bring the people to the saving knowledge of Christ and build them up as disciples of the Lord. You must take time to nurture, equip and disciple them for genuine Christian living and loving God with their whole heart. Your competence must show in your ability to lead the church to truly worship God in spirit and in truth.

You must also help the people to discover their gifts and ministry and release the saints to do the work of the ministry. If your relationship with the flock doesn't lead them to serve the Lord in sincerity and become ministers of the gospel that reach out to others, then you are not competent in this area yet.

6. Growing in relationship with the world.

You must be competent enough as a pastoral leader to relate well with the world around your ministry. That involves seeing the community as your parish, not only your four walls. You must be community conscious and project a good image in the locality. You must become socially responsible and lead the church to reach out to the community in kind and cash. Social efforts that soften hearts must be embarked upon by the church under your pastoral leadership. The church must meet needs and provide succor to the people of its immediate environ as much as finance will allow.

You must grow to become a community pastor – reaching out to people in the community with the love of Jesus, prayers, kind words and gifts. The church must give back to her host communities through developmental projects under your able leadership. Your competence must never be in doubt here, if you

Healthy Leaders, Healthy Churches

are going to be a leader to be reckoned with. The image you project in the community must be that of a true and genial servant of the Lord who is a blessing to all.

7. Growing in relationship with the word of God

Pastoral leaders must display high competence in the handling of the word of God. The word of God is the instrument of change that God has given to everyone of His leader. That is why the Apostle says, **"But we will give ourselves continually to prayer, and to the ministry of the word." (Acts 6:4).**

The increase of the word will be the increase of the church. You must not study the word just to preach, but you must discover biblical truths for personal edification first. Live it before you teach or preach it. It is then it will have power. **"Jesus began both to do and to teach."** (Acts 1:1).

Be a good example of your preaching and teaching. Practise good hermeneutics – balance interpretation and understanding of the scriptures. Preach and teach a wholistic gospel – not one sided truth that will eventually lead to extremes and error. Preach, not just to inform but to form lives. Grow in your understanding of the Bible through regular study, learning, taking courses and contextualizing the Bible to everyday situations of the

> *You must develop great competence and expertise in handling the word of God, it is only then you can build well-rounded work and people for the Lord and eternity.*

people. You must develop great competence and expertise in handling the word of God, it is only then you can build well-rounded work and people for the Lord and eternity.

"Study to show thyself approved unto God, a workman that needeth not to be ashamed, rightly dividing the word of truth." (II Timothy 2:15)

8. Growing in relevance and resourcefulness

You cannot afford to become redundant, stagnant and irrelevant as a pastoral leader. Rather, you must seek to grow in your relevance and resourcefulness. To be relevant, you must have a very strong prayer life. You must become a prayer warrior and literally live on your knees. You must fight to maintain a vital life of prayer and fellowship with the Lord. To be relevant, the presence and power of the Holy Spirit must be fresh and new in your life. Your anointing must never run dry nor grow stale. You must renew the anointing always.

To be resourceful, you must study, read, learn, take courses and continually go to school. You must gather materials, read books repeatedly and prepare resources for your teachings. Your competence will always depend on your relevance and resourcefulness.

Dry, drab and stale pastors will no longer elicit the support of people. You must keep investing in yourself. Because if you don't invest in yourself, people will no longer invest in you. You must keep updating, upgrading and uplifting yourself to new level of revelation, anointing and power as a result of your daily prayers, fasting, learning and anointing. Then, your relevance will not be in doubt and you will not be rejected.

9. Growing as a mentor, equipper and trainer

The goal of leadership is not to Lord over God's people, but to help them become all that God created them to be. You must become competent in this area too. You must engage in discovering and developing the gifts and grace of your people. You must have eyes that recognize potentials in others. You must be a developer of talents and discoverer of gifts. You must always be a lifter and not a limiter of people. Your associates, deacons, elders, committee members and workers must be given room and chance to express the deposits of God inside them.

You must be secure enough to allow others to rise and shine. You must relate well with your associates and under leaders. You must be generous with praise and miserly with criticism. Provide materials, books, resources and opportunities that will help them to rise and shine. It must not be difficult for you to release people to their God-given ministries and provide a soft landing for them. You must display expertise in raising lots of Timothy that will expand the frontiers of God's kingdom.

"And the things that thou hast heard of me among many witnesses, the same commit thou to faithful men, who shall be able to teach others also." (II Tim.2:2)

Your ministry is not complete if you don't invest in raising future leaders. You must mentor, equip and train others. All your ministry time should not be spent in praying, deliverance, counseling and healing people, but also in training, equipping and empowering young leaders. You must show expertise in raising leaders that will continue the vision and expand His kingdom. Discipleship manuals, teaching emphasis in the church and leadership development courses must be part and parcel of your ministerial portfolio.

10. Growing in communication ability

One crucial area you must show competence is your ability to communicate. No leader can lead well and long without becoming competent in the area of communication.

Communication starts from being credible enough to speak to the hearts of people. Your life and words must agree together. You must be dependable and trustworthy enough to be listened to. It is important that you work to become a good communicator, not just a speaker.

A speaker is concerned with his outline, while a communicator is concerned with the hearts of the people. A speaker wants to display knowledge while a communicator wants to touch lives.

> *Leaders must seek to rally people to a common objective through clear communication.*

To be a communicator, you must learn to speak in an interesting, relevant, humorous and lively way. You must seek to connect with the hearts of the people.

Using stories, illustrations, jokes, anecdotes and humor to reach the ears and hearts of people is a powerful way to communicate.

You are allowed to use creative ways to pass your message across, such as visuals, DVDs, bulletin and print outs. Leaders must grow in their communication skills. Leaders must seek to touch hearts of people with their words. Leaders must seek to rally people to a common objective through clear communication. You must be competent in this area.

"His disciples said unto him, lo, now speakest thou plainly, and speakest no proverb. Now are we sure that thou knowest all things, and needest not that any man should ask thee: by this we believe that thou camest forth from God." (John 16:29-30)

11. Growing in problem solving skills

Another name for ministry is problem. You will encounter problems and will be expected to handle and solve problems. Problems are part and parcel of church and ministry life. Sometimes, people are the problems.

Repeatedly, you will be called upon to handle and solve problems. Your inability to tackle them and display of fear, dread, cringing and shivering in the face of problems are pointers to your incompetence. You must realize the three facts about problems: you can't stop them from coming; you can't run away from them; but you can solve them.

It is important that you develop competence in handling and solving problems. Wrong and immature

Healthy Leaders, Healthy Churches

handling has aggravated many otherwise simple problems. Handling problems in a mature and admirable way shows your competence.

Your problem handling skills must continue to grow. You must learn to address issues, not personality. You must display courage, confidence and presence of mind in tackling issues. Learn to address them squarely, timely, promptly and decisively. Take the initiative and confront the problematic person without fear but love and understanding.

Every problem you solve gives people another reason to trust and follow your leadership. Providing solution to problems, either long term or fresh ones, will bring much credibility to your leadership. Your growing competence in handling and tackling problems with amicable solutions will convince your detractors.

12. Growing as a change agent

More than in any other area, pastoral leaders must show competence in bringing and managing change in the church. Growth, progress and health in the church calls for change. Nowhere will your leadership be more tested than in the area of change.

Change is the only constant thing in life. The church must change and move with changing times. If you don't welcome change in your life, you cannot bring it to the church. To be a change agent, you must change first. Change in those areas people are complaining about your life. Bring change to your life and then you can bring it to those you are leading.

Healthy Leaders, Healthy Churches

In the church, recognize church methods and tradition. Identify those dogmas and systems that can be changed. Take steps to communicate the needed change to influential people in the church and encourage worthwhile change that can bring progress and growth. Systematically bring change after times of teaching, sharing, praying and motivating people to see the great benefits that will be derived from the change.

Change must be gradual and progressive. Don't change too fast or too quickly, else those who are against change will move away. In the same vein, don't refuse to implement change, else, those who want change will also move away!

You can sustain the changes through your leadership credibility and positive results. And so long you pursue excellence in ministry; every change can be worthwhile and result-oriented. Your competence and expertise in bringing and managing change must be growing by the day. Your ministry and leadership must bring change to others. You must lead for change in all ramifications.

It remains to be said that it is absolutely impossible to become a competent pastoral leader in a day, month or a year. It is a time consuming and tedious process that you cannot cut short in anyway.

If you want to truly become a competent pastoral leader, then you must daily, monthly and yearly work on these twelve areas in your life. You must keep growing and improving in these areas until you are good and excellent at them. And that will take a serious and focused heart.

Healthy Leaders, Healthy Churches

    Don't forget, your competence in these areas will help your ministry in no small measure. Therefore, you must never settle for the average in any one of them. Decide to make the Holy Spirit your senior partner; seek to deepen your spiritual life always; embark on the journey of personal growth; improvement and development; sharpen your skills to lead; possess a learning spirit and pursue excellence in all you do.

    Remember, good is the enemy of better, better is the enemy of best and best is the enemy of excellence. Seek for excellence in leadership and your ministry will be a mighty force in the hand of God to change the world.

Healthy Leaders, Healthy Churches

INTERNATIONAL CHURCH GROWTH MINISTRIES

International Church Growth Ministries was founded in 1994. The vision of the ministry is to provide current and reliable Church Growth principles in African context to Leaders, Pastors and Ministers that will lead to better and faster growth of their churches.

We do these through books, materials, VCD and audio cassettes at relatively low cost to people engaged in leading the church.

We equally organise seminars and conferences on various aspect of Church Growth and Health. We also accept invitations from churches to help analyse them, motivate their people and generally help the growth potentials of churches.

So far we have ministered to over 20,000 Pastors and Christian Workers across many denominational lines and independent churches. The results have been tremendous and the testimonies have been wonderful and interesting.

The ministry also saw the need to really raise the growth consciousness in the Continent and decided to pioneer an Institute on Church Growth. The response has been overwhelming as so many Pastors, General Overseers, and Church Leaders have enrolled to learn more about how to practically lead their churches to growth. The impact of the Institute on these Pastors' lives have started manifesting in the phenomenal growth of their churches and expansion of their ministries.

Healthy Leaders, Healthy Churches

ICGM RESOURCES

If you found this book to be useful, you may be interested in some of the other resources available from ICGM.

Listed below are some of our books and resources:

Books:

1. 40 Strategic Ways to Increase Church attendance
2. Supernatural Power, Miracles, Signs & Wonders Today
3. Your Growth is Your Future
4. The Secrets of Financially Strong Churches
5. Our Churches and His Church
6. Why Churches Breakaway & Lose members
7. Strategic Living
8. Leading Your Church to Lasting Growth
9. 22 Dynamic Laws of Church Growth
10. Strategic Church Planting Today
11. How to Support and Strengthen Your Pastors

Healthy Leaders, Healthy Churches

12. Leading From the Pulpit
13. Spiritual Warfare for Dynamic Church Growth
14. The Place of Anointing and Administration
15. Family Growth
66. Prayer Nugget
17. Church Growth
18. Financial Growth
19. The Impact Driven Church
20. Grow the Pastor, Grow the Church
21. Personal Growth Today
22. The Loyal Associate
23. Fruitful and Fulfilling Ministry Today
24. Quality and Quantity Growth In Churches
25. Sexual Purity In Leadership
26. Money, Ministers & Ministry Today
27. Guest Ministers Today

Resources:
a. Spiritual Warfare for church growth
b. Helping the clergy - leading your church to growth.
c. Practical church planting
d. Winning the society seminar
e. Mobilizing the laity
f. Warfare prayer for Growth
g. Closing the Backdoor of the church
h. Women ministry in church growth
i. Strategic level prayer for breakthrough
j. Signs and Wonders for church growth
k. Research and analysing of the church
l. How to grow a vibrant and Healthy churches
m. Why Churches Lose Members
n. Empowering the Church for 21st Century
o. Healthy Leadership for Healthy Churches
p. Tools for Tremendous and Transforming Ministry.
q. New Waves of God's Move for End Time Harvest

Healthy Leaders, Healthy Churches

r. Magnetic, Multiplying, Marketable and Maximum Impact.
s. Building a Bigger, Better and Broader Church and many others.

Audio Tapes, CD & VCD
1. Spiritual Warfare Series
2. Effective Ministers Series
3. Women Ministry Series
4. Closing the Backdoor Series
5. Warfare Prayer Series
6. Strategic Level Prayer Series
7. Church Planting Series
8. Healthy Church Series.

Journal:
Church Growth Journal is a quarterly teaching and news magazine that gives vital and practical information on how to grow the church.

For further information on these and other resources available, please write or contact us at our office or call the telephone lines provided in this book.

SECRETS OF FINANCIALLY STRONG CHURCHES
By: Francis Bola Akin-John

Do you still have problem raising money to effectively run your ministry or church? Or do you lack proper knowledge on how to manage it to achieve financial freedom for the church? Then this book is for you. It answers your questions about money, tells you why people give or don't give in your church and also offers practical solution to grow a debt - free and financially robust ministry. A must for you if you passionately desire financial buoyancy for your church.

22 DYNAMIC LAWS OF CHURCH GROWTH
By: Francis Bola Akin-John

Church growth is not a logical programme. It is a dynamic process made possible by strict adherence to various laws that guide durable, lasting and solid growth in the church. Violating any of these laws will cause retrogression and stagnation in the church, but an understanding of the laws enumerated in this well researched book will not only ensure growth in your church but it will also sustain the growth in any season. This book is a classic work and still one of the best materials from Africa's foremost Church Growth and Ministerial Consultant, by Francis Bola Akin-John.

YOUR GROWTH IS YOUR FUTURE
By: Francis Bola Akin-John

Growth has no alternative. It is not optional. Your growth is your vehicle to the future. Your growth determines the level you will get to in life. If you desire success passionately either as a pastor, businessman or woman, student, corporate leader, trader, church worker, professional, house wife or church leader, this book is for you. Your personal growth precedes every other growth. Without growth you will become a person of yesterday, abort your greater future and open door for decay. This is a book for everybody.

SUPERNATURAL POWER, MIRACLES, SIGNS AND WONDERS TODAY
By: Francis Bola Akin-John

Many of the great growth of churches today are closely linked with the supernatural dimension of God. Without doubt, these are the days of God's power like never before. Every church and leader must key in to the supernatural move of God, if true and lasting church growth is to be seen and experienced.

This book by Dr. Francis Bola Akin-John re-establishes the truth that every church leader can and should display the power of God's kingdom over that of the enemy. Church leaders and ministers that really desire to operate in the supernatural realm of God must not only read, but also digest, study and soak up this book.

40 STRATEGIC WAYS TO INCREASE CHURCH ATTENDANCE
By: Francis Bola Akin-John

Church growth isn't automatic! It is achieved through the combination of spiritual, physical and environmental factors. By indepth research, coupled with rich personal experience as a pastor for many years, Dr. Akin-John highlights diverse strategies for numerical increase and growth in the church. If you read this book and prayerfully implement its content, you will discover that strategy is always better than energy. Get this book if you desire a passionate increase in your attendance. A must for every pastor!

STRATEGIC CHURCH PLANTING TODAY
By: Francis Bola Akin-John

The last two decade witnessed an unprecedented church planting efforts by various Christian denominations, mission- minded individuals and independent ministers. In this book, Dr. Akin-John, himself a researcher on church and ministerial matters, chronicles these efforts and examines the need, method, cost implication, the passion, the benefits, mistakes, misconception, planning, timing, impact, location, the message and the messenger of church planting today. No one has approached church planting than the way this book has done. It is a vintage material fro

SPIRITUAL WARFARE FOR DYNAMIC CHURCH GROWTH
By: Francis Bola Akin-John

Achieving outstanding growth in your church is determined by how sharp your attacking instruments of warfare are. The war for control over the territory where your church is located must start in the spirit and end in the spirit. To have peace in your life, family and ministry, you must prepare for war. You must enforce growth and increase by violence in the spirit through all levels of spiritual warfare. Dr. Bola Akin-John made the subject matter more practical than theory here, with strong warning that harvest will tarry in your church unless you are willing to go all out against the visible and invisible power s of the enemy.

GROW THE PASTOR
GROW THE CHURCH
By: Francis Bola Akin-John

The pastor is the number one key to the growth of the church. The pastor must be trained for maximum impact making in the church. An ungroomed pastor is much more dangerous to the church than the church is to him. This is because the church will be strong if the pastor is strong, the church will be prayerful if the pastor is prayerful, the church will be holy if the pastor is holy, the church will be weak if the pastor is weak and the church will grow if the pastor is growing. This book must not be missing in your library if you are a pastor that has other pastors or leaders within your leadership scope.

LEADING YOUR CHURCH TO LASTING GROWTH
By: Francis Bola Akin-John

Much more than the influx of people into your church and the excitement of ministering to a large crowd, this book unfolds to you powerful strategies necessary to sustain the growth.
Dr. Akin-John goes further to share with you time and field tested biblical principles that will ensure lasting growth and increase in your church.

HOW TO SUPPORT AND STRENGTHEN YOUR PASTOR
By: Francis Bola Akin-John

No church can grow and experience all round increase without the faithful and collective contributions of her members. Unfortunately, many Christians know next to nothing about how to uphold and support their pastors. Here, the author spells out the responsibilities of every church member, associate leaders and heads of various church departments to their pastor - knowing fully well that what makes a good pastor is often the support of good people around him.

THE IMPACT DRIVEN CHURCH
By: Francis Bola Akin-John

The church is the only designated God's property on the surface of the earth. It was birthed to meet human needs and stand in the gap between man and God. Any church that does not align with this position can not make impact in this end time. Your church must make impact in the environment where it is located in order to be relevant in the community. It must stop existing as a mere figure but a force. In this book, Dr. Francis Bola Akin-John discusses with you how to make impact and be driven by same.

WHY CHURCHES BREAKAWAY AND LOSE MEMBERS
By: Francis Bola Akin-John

The rate at which churches breakaway is almost the same rate churches are being planted. The problem has grown to endemic proportions in the last couple of years, affecting every church either old or new. As a foremost Consultant on ministry and church matters, the author examines the causes of breakaway and membership loses in churches and proffers lasting solutions that will arrest chaos, retrogression, split and membership loses. This is a book every church Founder, General Overseer, Apostle, Superintendent, State and Regional Pastor, Senior Pastor and whoever intends to start a fresh work should r

GUEST MINISTERS TODAY
By: Francis Bola Akin-John

The reality is that no minister or leader, no matter how anointed or close to God he is, can build and run a ministry or lead a church alone. He will always need the gift and ministry of others in his work. The truth, however, is that guest ministers have the capacity to make or mar his work.

How to handle the issue of guest ministers in the church and ministry so as not to hinder her growth but help it is the focus of this book by Dr. Francis Bola Akin-John.

GUEST MINISTERS TODAY is a must for both guest ministers and host ministers

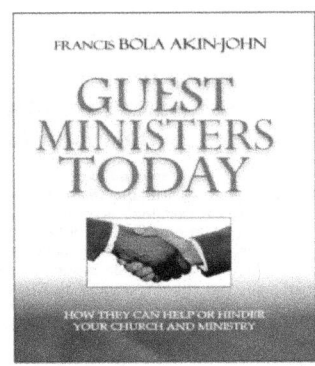

OUR CHURCHES AND HIS CHURCH
By: Francis Bola Akin-John

This book is an attempt to put a hand on the crisis that has engulfed the church today. Many practices, methods and models have clearly shown that our 'churches' are not necessarily His church. Many of what we call 'church' today are too far from what Christ had in mind when He said; "I will build my church ". Likewise, many of the people in 'churches' today cannot be said to be His people simply because majority of them do not really know Him. Therefore, if you are really concerned about building His church, and you want to do a work that will not get burnt up, this book is for you! Every Senior Pastor, Bishop, General Overseer and Pastor must read this book over and over again and change where necessary.

LEADING FROM THE PULPIT
By: Francis Bola Akin-John

The pulpit ministry is the most profound and glamorous ministry of any pastor. It represents the power, glory, purpose, authority, unction, influence, mandate, character, growth and communicative ability of the pastor. Here, Dr. Akin-John brings to bear his years of experience arising from close interaction, teaching and training of pastors and church leaders on church growth principles for a decade now and shows you a world of difference between preaching and leading from the pulpit. Read this all important book and position yourself for expansion, revival and growth in your church.

FRUITFUL AND FULFILLING MINISTRY TODAY
By: Francis Bola akin-John

This book is a tool that will help your ministry to move to the next level. Your ministry is the vehicle you are driving, you need tools to keep it running effectively and fast.
The quickness and durability of your ministry is determined by the tools of ministry at your disposal. Tools will help you to be effective, result oriented, impactful, creative, fruitful and to have tremendous and transforming ministry.
Those tools are scattered throughout in this book. Grab the ones you need by reading, studying, digesting and practising the insights in the book, so that you will no longer work as fools. It is only fools that lack real, genuine, relevant and creative tools for life and ministry.

THE LOYAL ASSOCIATE
By: Francis Bola Akin-John

This book is Dr. Francis bola Akin-John humble effort at establishing a right type of relationship between the leader and his associates, providing the right atmosphere for it and bringing sanity into the ungodly madness of unfaithful, disloyal and undependable associates.
It is appropriate for topmost leaders, useful and insightful for those in the middle leadership and challenging to those at the lowest rung of the ladder. If you can adapt and adjust to the timely truth of this book, you will save yourself from many hurts and heartaches.

PERSONAL GROWTH TODAY
By: Francis Bola akin-John

Dr. Francis Bola Akin-John in this book revealed that the gap between a person's vision and present reality can only be filled through commitment to his personal development. And that personal growth prevents personal and professional stagnation, and surely impacts organisational growth. If you want to reach the height of your potential, personally and professionally, then commit yourself to daily personal improvement.
Personal Growth Today is a classic that must not be missed. Read, study and digest this book over and over again. Drink deep from it and let it become part and parcel of your daily living.

QUALITY AND QUANTITY GROWTH IN CHURCHES
By: Francis Bola Akin-John

What is the condition of your church? Is it of high or low quality? What kind of work are you doing for the Lord? Will it stand the test of fire? You can ask and answer these questions honestly now and make amend reading this book: Quality and Quantity Growth in Churches by Dr. Francis Bola Akin-John.
This book is for those heavenly minded and eternity-conscious leaders who do not want to suffer loss or labour in vain and be put to shame on the last day. Get it and use it as a mirror to examine whether you have been doing church according to God's standard or your own set measurement.

SEXUAL PURITY IN LEADERSHIP
By: Francis Bola Akin-John

Sexual pressure is one pressure no leader or minister can escape in life and ministry. Unfortunately, the devil has succeeded in using the weapon of sex to ruin and incapacitate many once great servants of the Lord. Many great evangelists, preachers, pastors, bishops and church leaders have lost their anointing and ministry on the laps of strange women.
Sexual Purity in Leadership by Dr. Francis Bola Akin-John exposes the destructive and deadly sexual traps employ by satan against leaders and ministers of God and provides ways to avoid them. The earlier you are properly informed about it, the better for you. Get this book NOW!

MONEY, MINISTERS & MINISTRY TODAY
By: Francis Bola Akin-John

Many of the books on money in print have failed to strike the needed balance for gospel ministers. Much of the teachings on finance appeal to secular audience. Therefore, many ministers of the gospel are at a loss on how to really make, manage and multiply money for kingdom purposes.
MONEY, MINISTERS & MINISTRY TODAY is written to bring the needed change and balance to the issue of money in the ministry today. It provides the information needed by ministers to examine their lifestyles and attitude towards money and make amends where necessary.
Get this book, read with open mind and get financial freedom for your life and ministry.

THE PLACE OF ANOINTING & ADMINISTRATION IN CHURCH GROWTH
By Dr. Francis Bola Akin-John

The sustainable growth of the church of Jesus Christ have been gravely affected by wrong notions on the dual issue of ANOINTING and ADMINISTRATION. It has been discovered that there is lack of balance in the church as regards each of these two areas.
The principles highlighted in this powerful book provide the needed balanced approach on the issue of anointing and administration.
A must read book for every minister! Read it for your edification and practise it for your promotion.

25 PILLARS OF CHURCH HEALTH
By Dr. Francis Bola Akin-John

Large crowds and fine buildings do not necessarily make for healthy churches. There are too many of such churches that are physically and materially okay, but are sick, diseased and rotten up internally. The truth is that church growth and health must go together. Churches can start from growth and gradually move to health. But both must be held in constant tension in the church.
It is not enough to have a church, we must do everything scripturally possible to make that church a healthy one. Every serious church leader must read, study, digest, dissect and discover those gems that will make his or her church a healthy one.

CHURCH CHANGE
By Dr. Francis Bola Akin-John

The world has undergone tremendous changes in the last 30 years more than any other time. The church is in the midst of a changing world. In a nutshell, the church must welcome and embrace change, if she is to make lasting impact in the world.
The desire of Dr. Francis Bola Akin-John to see balanced and positive changes in the church of today, so that the world will be won for Christ necessitate the writing of this book.
The benefits of the book: Church Change are enormous, if the truth therein are embraced and adapted by every church leader.

www.ingramcontent.com/pod-product-compliance
Lightning Source LLC
Chambersburg PA
CBHW032004060426
42449CB00031B/277